Loving in a Time of Exile

CAC *Publishing*

Center for Action and Contemplation
cac.org

"*Oneing*" is an old English word that was used by Lady Julian of Norwich (1342-1416) to describe the encounter between God and the soul. The Center for Action and Contemplation proudly borrows the word to express the divine unity that stands behind all of the divisions, dichotomies, and dualisms in the world. We pray and publish with Jesus' words, "that all may be one" (John 17:21).

EDITOR:
Mark Longhurst

ASSOCIATE EDITOR:
Shirin McArthur

PUBLISHER:
The Center for Action and Contemplation

ADVISORY BOARD:
David Benner
James Danaher
Ilia Delio, OSF
Sheryl Fullerton
Stephen Gaertner, OPraem

Layout by Caleb Allison and artwork by Izzy Spitz

© 2025 Center for Action and Contemplation.
All rights reserved.

Oneing

VOLUME 13 NO. 1

EDITOR'S NOTE 5

BRIAN D. MCLAREN
Islands of Sanity 7

CARMEN ACEVEDO BUTCHER
A Hospitable Soul and a Well-Said Word in a Hostile Time 15

MIRABAI STARR
Luminous Darkness 21

PAUL SWANSON
The Monastic Impulse Leads to Unintentional Menageries in Love 29

BARBARA C. OTERO-LÓPEZ
Listen 37

PAMELA AYO YETUNDE
My Exile Trilogy 43

ROSEMERRY WAHTOLA TROMMER
Letter to the Parts of Me I Have Tried to Exile 51

BELDEN LANE
The Countercultural Spirituality of the Desert Christians 53

CONNIE ZWEIG
    The Holy Longing   59

OR N. ROSE
    Abraham Joshua Heschel: Moral Grandeur
    and Spiritual Audacity   67

MICHAEL BATTLE
    A Holy Exile   73

RANDY S. WOODLEY
    Never Alone   81

LEE STAMAN
    Borders and Belonging: The Book of Ruth:
    A Story for Our Times   89

CONTRIBUTORS   93

NOTES   97

EDITOR'S NOTE

Some of the most inspired people and movements in the Christian contemplative tradition experienced the pain of personal or collective exile. The short letter of 1 Peter, tucked away at the end of the New Testament, begins: "To the exiles of the dispersion . . . may grace and peace be yours in abundance" (1 Peter 1:1). The letter's readers saw themselves as Christians exiled from the larger Roman imperial political machine, but they still saw their vocation as embodying "grace and peace." As CAC Dean of Faculty Brian McLaren points out in his passionate and wise article, authoritarian regimes exile those who do not conform. Contemplation in both biblical times and our times becomes a necessary survival strategy to help us resist conformity.

The third-century Desert Fathers and Mothers did just that—they formed countercultural exile communities. Theologian Belden Lane, whose desert-spirituality classic *The Solace of Fierce Landscapes* is excerpted in this issue, writes about how their single-minded devotion to God cultivated an indifference to the "social and political preoccupations of a compulsive world." Carmen Acevedo Butcher tells us about how, in the sixth century, Benedict of Nursia also chose the lure of exiled prayer in the desert, forming communities who banded together around a common "Rule of Life." Mirabai Starr writes of Spanish mystic John of the Cross's imprisonment by fellow Carmelite monks and how he channeled his exiled longings for the Divine Beloved into love poetry.

Contemporary figures Desmond Tutu and Abraham Joshua Heschel powerfully incarnated the divine love that does not exile any person. Michael Battle highlights how Tutu's contemplative spirituality demonstrated such non-exiling love through nonviolent direct action in opposing South Africa's apartheid regime. In the United States, Abraham Joshua Heschel's Jewish faith and study of the Hebrew prophets propelled him to "pray with his feet," marching from Selma to Montgomery for voting rights in 1965 with the Rev. Dr. Martin Luther King Jr.

Collective and personal exiles overlap. Alongside following a compassionate call to support those rendered exiles by intentional public policy, Pamela Ayo Yetunde shares the pain of suffering exile from her family due to her sexual identity, and the liberating love she experienced in a like-spirited community of exiles. CAC Programs Director Barb Lopez shares how searching the "sacred geography" of her ancestors' Indigenous roots revealed the trauma of colonization but also a resilient love that can inspire us today. Poet Rosemerry Wahtola Trommer generously wrote an original poem for this *Oneing* issue in which she welcomes home parts of herself that she had tried to exile.

There are parts within each of us that we banish out of shame, woundedness, fear, and inherited family system patterns. There are systems of power around us that exile those who are different or do not comply. The articles and authors in this issue invite us to rediscover the God who exiles nothing and in whom all reality belongs.

Mark Longhurst
Editor, *Oneing*

Islands of Sanity

By Brian D. McLaren

Authoritarian regimes are generally not very creative. Their methods follow a tired old pattern, a predictable repetition of the same-old same-old.

Hannah Arendt (1906–1975) was one of the first and clearest to describe the pattern. In 1951, in *The Origins of Totalitarianism*, she wrote, "Before mass leaders seize the power to fit reality to their lies, their propaganda is marked by its extreme contempt for facts as such, for in their opinion fact depends entirely on the power of man who can fabricate it."[1]

Right-wing political activist/propagandist Steve Bannon memorably captured Arendt's insight in a 2018 interview. He said, "The Democrats don't matter. The real opposition is the media. And the way to deal with them is to flood the zone with sh*t."[2]

The pattern is oft-repeated because it works. It works especially well in our contemporary world of social media, where we have multiple zones with millions of propagandists eager to pour out lies, deception, and other forms of fecality.

When people are flooded with misinformation, they don't know what to think, so they suspend thinking. They just consume "content," judging it for how interesting or clever it is, having lost the ability to discern whether it is true, half-true, or false.

Meanwhile, they must keep acting and living, so they live and act without serious thought: consuming, liking, subscribing, consuming more.

We have a number of words to describe living without coherent thought: madness, foolishness, insanity.

How do we survive in a time when hurricane-force deception and madness levels are reaching flood stage?

One answer might surprise you: *contemplation*.

For people facing a flood of madness, contemplation becomes not a luxury, but rather a survival strategy. Contemplation is a way of sequestering our attention from the floods of propaganda and misinformation in which we swim these days (on top of normal levels of advertising, amusement, and gossip). By pulling away into solitude and descending into silence, we allow ourselves to recenter, recalibrate, and cleanse our mental palate with a sweet sip of holy silence. For those of us in the Christian tradition, we withdraw from the public world of propaganda and allow ourselves to rest, to bathe, to marinate in the presence of divine truth, love, wonder, and joy.

In this way, solitary contemplation becomes the doorway into communion—communion with the Spirit in whom we find a new relationship with ourselves, with others, with history, and with the cosmos.

In this way, contemplation may start in silence and solitude, but it never stops there. Especially in times of crisis, when truth is drowning in a flood of fecality, we are drawn from contemplative solitude into contemplative community. We find ourselves hungry for communion with others who are also seeking to live examined, mindful lives, to pull aside with even two or three mindful people for deep, honest fellowship. We might come together to sit in silence for a period of time or take a walk together, letting the shushing of our feet passing through autumn leaves hush the noise of a million monkey-minds clacking to the beat of a million keyboards, hankering for our attention. Or perhaps, before eating together, we cook together, turning the focus of our minds away from bitter political arguments and deceptive propaganda and turning together toward the simple savor of salt and potatoes, celery and bread, applesauce and wine.

When even two or three of us gather in the name of truth, honesty, and love, in the name of courage, compassion, and kindness, we find ourselves feeling joined by another presence–the presence of Christ, the way, the truth, and the life. We listen to one another with compassion and curiosity. We speak to one another with wisdom and wonder. We turn together toward the light. And that helps us create islands of sanity in a world that is losing its mind.

For people facing a flood of madness, contemplation becomes not a luxury, but rather a survival strategy.

Why does the authoritarian playbook repeatedly work so well? I suspect it works for two reasons. First, we humans share biases, glitches in our thinking that render us vulnerable to authoritarian leaders who substitute confidence for character and threats for truth. (I've written about these biases in two short ebooks and explored them in the "Learning How to See" podcast.[3]) The authoritarian playbook continues to work for a second reason as well. According to research by Canadian social psychologist Bob Altemeyer (and many others), about a third of people around the world qualify as authoritarian personalities. They respond to stress, shame, and danger by wishing for a strong man who will promise to fix everything and solve all problems if we just give him permission to break the rules (and perhaps break some bones of a real or imagined enemy) on our behalf.

Often, religious communities become aggregators where authoritarian leaders seek authoritarian followers who are seeking authoritarian leaders. Once religious authoritarian leaders aggregate religious authoritarian followers, they can present them to a political authoritarian leader in exchange for the attractive rewards of power, protection, and prestige.

In this way, the original thirty percent of authoritarian followers only need to win over twenty-one more percent of us in order to turn our democracies into tools for authoritarian regimes.

Once a majority has been won over to an authoritarian ideology, whether it is called National Socialism, Maoism, or Leninism, whether it's called Radical Islam or Christian or Hindu Nationalism, it becomes harder and harder to resist being swept along with the majority.

An expert in authoritarian regimes, Sarah Kenzior, captures the danger like this:

> Authoritarianism is not merely a matter of state control, it is something that eats away at who you are. It makes you afraid, and fear can make you cruel. It compels you to conform and to comply and accept things that you would never accept, to do things you never thought you would do.[4]

No wonder, in a time of authoritarian Caesar-worship, the early Christian leader Paul wrote, "Do not be conformed to this world. But be transformed by the renewal of your minds" (Romans 12:2). Kendzior addresses this very need for inner renewal and transformation. Authoritarian regimes, she says,

> Can take everything from you in material terms—your house, your job, your ability to speak and move freely. They cannot take away who you truly are. They can never truly know you, and that is your power.
>
> But to protect and wield this power, you need to know yourself—right now, before their methods permeate, before you accept the obscene and unthinkable as normal.[5]

Although she doesn't use the word *contemplation*, Kendzior points to the importance of knowing who we are, centering into what Howard Thurman called "the sound of the genuine" inside us. She continues,

> We are heading into dark times, and you need to be your own light. Do not accept brutality and cruelty as normal even if it is sanctioned. Protect the vulnerable and encourage the afraid. If you are brave, stand up for others. If you cannot be brave—and it is often hard to be brave—be kind. But most of all, never lose sight of who you are and what you value.[6]

I am thinking about these authoritarian patterns not only to better understand what's happening now in my country. I'm also trying to understand my own country's history—how millions of so-called Christians in America consented to the genocide of indigenous peoples and then consented to the enslavement of kidnapped and trafficked Africans and then consented to American apartheid in the Jim Crow era and then resisted the civil rights movement.

Contemplative practices help us resist conformity with wisdom and courage.

Studying biases and authoritarianism is also helping me understand in a deeper way why contemplative practices, and especially contemplative practices in community, are so important right now.

Contemplative practices are many things. Our Christian tradition teaches us that they are pathways into the direct experience of divine presence and love. Contemporary neuroscience adds that they are also pathways into self-regulation. I suspect that sociologists could also see them as resistance strategies against the predictable patterns of authoritarianism.

Authoritarian regimes and totalitarian systems try to train everyone's thoughts to move along the same ironclad tracks, and they punish public departure—often brutally. Contemplative practices—both solitary and communal—help us resist conformity with wisdom and courage.

Contemplative mindfulness helps us resist the authoritarian mindlessness that comes from zones being flooded with disinformation, and it helps us resist being loaded onto authoritarian trains of thought that always lead to the same place: more power for the powerful and more harm for everyone else.

Lately, I've been thinking about how engaged contemplative community helps us "be transformed by the renewal of our minds" in four specific and powerful ways:

First, authoritarians consistently put us on dualistic tracks, where everything is *us versus them*. But through engaged contemplative community, we move from dualism (us versus them) to holism (all of us, in this together).

Second, authoritarians squeeze us onto narrow, linear tracks of simplistic cause and effect. But through engaged contemplative community, our thinking broadens to engage with complex systems. Through network thinking and systems thinking, we can look at multiple conditions that lead to cascading effects rather than single causes that lead to single effects.

Third, authoritarians typically pressure us to conform to a strict conventional morality. This morality tends to be rule-based and outcome-based, and it tends to favor those in power and deny or minimize the harm done to everyone else. But the contemplative mind and heart lead us toward a deeper morality, a prophetic way of being that seeks equal justice for all, that unseats conventional supremacies, and that is willing to speak truth to Pharaohs and Nebuchadnezzars and Caesars, whenever and wherever they appear.

And fourth, authoritarians typically instigate chaos and fear so that we are put in a constant reactive mode, which leaves us in a perpetual state of exhaustion. But contemplative community invites us into an intentional mode, where we choose how we want to show up—not bearing the fruits of reactivity but rather the fruits of the Spirit.

When two or three contemplatives create zones of nonconformity in this way, they create what sociologists call a plausibility structure, a social space where there is permission to think differently, to feel differently, to be and live differently. In these autonomous zones, the regime does not rule, so people can dance to songs of joy rather than march to the drumbeats of war. They can speak their spontaneous thanks to the Creator rather than parrot sycophantic praise to the rulers. They can embrace one another as family, regardless of race, ethnicity, gender, social class, or religion, rather than examine one another for patriotic, ideological, or doctrinal purity.

Unsurprisingly, once a few gather in these communities of convergence (to use Parker Palmer's beautiful term), others often come out of the shadows. Soon, two or three become five or ten, fifty or five hundred. Rather than being confused or pressured to conform by political propaganda or algorithms designed by billionaires for billionaires, these little flocks can easily become movements of freedom. They can engage in mutual support that not only helps people survive for another day in the present regime, but also helps people dream of a better day beyond this regime. They can even begin to embody a new way of life in their common life together.

The uglier the general culture becomes, the more beautiful these countercultural communities become. While authoritarian regimes persist in the same-old same-old, members of contemplative communities dare to believe that God is doing a new thing.

And they dare to sing a new song.

If you would like to bring together two or three or more for an experiment in engaged contemplative community, you can find resources through the Center for Courage & Renewal: https://couragerenewal.org/courage-renewal-approach/. You may also wish to explore the CAC's "Essentials of Engaged Contemplation" course, which launches in September 2025.

A Hospitable Soul and a Well-Said Word in a Hostile Time

By Carmen Acevedo Butcher

The Psalms are our Bread of Heaven in the wilderness of our Exodus.

–Thomas Merton[1]

At the age of twentysomething, Benedict of Nursia (480–547) walked into a cave that would change his world. But before he became a quiet countercultural leader in his day and was later named the father of Western monasticism, Benedict began life squarely in the mainstream.

Born *liberiori genere*, "of good birth," he grew up in a wealthy Roman family in a small hill village in Umbria, Italy's beautiful central region.[2] He spent his childhood among its olive groves, vineyards, cypress woods, lavender bushes, cherry orchards, mulberry trees, and tall Apennines. Centuries later, these inspired fellow Umbrian Francis of Assisi (1182–1226) to write "Brother Sun, Sister Moon," celebrating sacred kinship and interdependence with creation.[3]

As a teenager, Benedict moved to Rome with his family. In its classical schools, he must have studied politician-orator Cicero's plays, speeches, essays, rhetorical works, and epigrams; Stoic philosopher Seneca's works; and others. He also encountered a world where wealthy students lounged on couches and indulged in Roman cultural excesses like the marathon three-course dinner, copious wine, delicacies like roasted peacock, stuffed figs for dessert, and entertainment by dancing young women. The Roman poet Horace provided a glimpse into such feasters, saying they ate "like wild pigs."[4]

Most people in Italy, however, had a very different life. Long afflicted by the Roman Empire's rigid caste system, they suffered even more intensely as the empire was collapsing. Waves of invaders were devastating society, as were displacements, homelessness, plague, famine, drought, and a volcanic winter that began in 536 CE.[5]

But young Benedict's culturally successful trajectory seemed certain. His Roman father or *paterfamilias* would have had plans and demands, and his son, as part of society's in-groups, would have been expected to leverage social position for a career in law or politics.

At this point, however, a stirring in Benedict moved him to choose the uncertainty of self-exile and contemplation in a world of collective exile and traumatization. Benedict left school, home, wealth, inheritance, status, and the potential comforts of marriage to follow a new path, "desiring only to please God": "*soli Deo placere cupiens*,"[6] as Gregory the Great (540–604) told in *Dialogues*, Book Two, the only ancient account of Benedict's life.

First, Benedict walked over forty miles east to Enfide, today's Affile. He performed his first miracle while living there. When Benedict's housekeeper came to him distraught, having broken a costly, borrowed *capisterium* (a kitchen sifter for winnowing wheat), Benedict prayed over the clay pieces, and it became whole.[7]

News of this miracle spread and brought him unlooked-for local fame. So, he walked further into solitude, two-and-a-half miles north, arriving in Sublaqueum, now Subiaco, so-called for its location "below the lakes" created by Roman gravity dams. Centuries before, Emperor Nero had his imperial summer residence here beside his expensive, man-made pleasure lakes.

A stirring in Benedict moved him to choose the uncertainty of self-exile and contemplation in a world of collective exile and traumatization.

Fortuitously, Benedict made a new friend here, the monk Romanus. He showed the aspiring hermit a ten-foot-deep cave positioned five hundred feet up a cliff. High above the lakes, it was not too far below the clifftop community where Romanus lived. He also promised to keep the young man's location a secret.

Benedict spent three years in the cave, meditating and eating herbs and whatever simple food Romanus lowered to him on a rope. In this voluntary poverty, wearing animal-skin garb and practicing what James Finley calls "a daily rendezvous with God,"[8] the once toga-clad Roman nobleman's son began to resemble a John the Baptist.

And again, Benedict was found out. People visited him, asking for a sage word. He began embodying the meaning of his name, for *Benedict* means, "well-said word; speak well, bless."

After a few twists and turns, including an attempted poisoning by some monastic brothers, Benedict felt the time had come to leave his cave in Subiaco and house those coming to see him regularly. He built twelve monasteries, each with twelve monks and a superior, whom he chose. He added a thirteenth monastery for those he felt would benefit from being mentored by him as abbot.

As Michael Petrow observes, Benedict's monasteries were "the bomb shelters, time capsules, laboratories, and protected cultivators of the contemplative tradition in a world falling apart."[9] They preserved the wisdom of the desert *ammas* and *abbas* and were communities of healing in a time of chaos.

Benedict's reputation for kind wisdom always attracted people from all backgrounds. He took in shepherd and high-born, immigrant and native, illiterate and educated, and young, middle-aged, and old. As violent, dehumanizing forces raged, he and his diverse communities chose to welcome strangers.

As one example, Gregory described Benedict's gentle pastoral care for a worried monastic brother who had once been an outsider as a Goth (an invading tribe that raided Italy). One day, as this conscientious monk was mowing, he lost a valuable iron scythe blade that suddenly came loose and flew from its handle, landing with a splash and sinking in a lake beside him. Instead of sending a messenger to investigate and console, Abbot Benedict went himself. Coming alongside this brother, he listened and reassured him not to worry.

We can learn much from Benedict. During societal disorder and crushing need, how did he sustain both his own and communal peace and compassionate activity? And how did the work of this obscure monk grow to have such an outsized influence today?

Richard Rohr's allegorical adaptation of Archimedes' law of the lever, in *A Lever and a Place to Stand*, can be applied to and can deepen our appreciation of Benedict, who repeatedly chose to live in and from the "fixed point" of a contemplative stance. In this calm place of daily *ora*—Psalm-chanting and Scripture-steeping *lectio divina*—Benedict stood "steady, centered, poised, and rooted," gaining "a slight distance from the world" even as his heart or fulcrum of engagement was "quite close to the world, . . . loving it, feeling its pains and its joys" as his own. In prayer, Benedict experienced a "detachment from the . . . useless distractions, and the daily delusions of the false self" that gave his fulcrum, set in the suffering of wrecked empire, the capacity to "move the world" through various "levers" of compassionate action, or *labora*, synonymous with being and becoming.[10]

Focused daily on doing the ordinary, Benedict's life was a series of risings in the dark. Most Italians, even bakers, were sound asleep when lights fired up in his monasteries before 2 a.m. in winter, as Benedict's community woke and walked to chapel for Vigils. They sang Psalm 51:15: *"Domine, labia mea aperies, et os meum annuntiabit laudem tuam"* / "Lord, open my lips, and my mouth will declare your praise." By 5 a.m., he had spent three hours engaged in communal prayer and chanting of Psalms, called the *Opus Dei*, the "work of God," or *Divine Office*.

Benedict prioritized this chanting through the 150 Psalms each week as a community, as his communities and descendants, Cistercians and Trappist monks, do today. The Desert Elder Athanasius (c. 300–373) described the daily hours spent singing Psalms as beneficial in teaching biblical history and prophecy, nurturing and maturing the emotions, and transforming how the chanter understands the Bible's words and even God: "The person who hears the Psalms as they sing them is deeply moved and changed by their words. They become a mirror where you see your soul. Whatever causes us grief is healed when we sing Psalms, and whatever causes us stumbling will be discovered. It's like the Psalms were written by you yourself. They become your own songs."[11] Thomas Merton (1915–1968) added: "The Psalms are more than language. They contain within themselves the silence of high mountains and the silence of heaven."[12]

Is the stranger within me and outside of me treated as the honored guest or the hated enemy?

During a time of instability and exiling, Benedict also crafted a grounding and open-hearted book—his *Rule*. At under 100 pages and with hundreds of biblical allusions, we might ask how it became so impactful. He wrote not for theologians and scholars, but primarily for his diverse monks, creating a practical guide on living out the Gospel in community. He wrote for all, calling it a "little rule . . . for beginners." An ancient saying captures its enduring appeal: "A lamb can bathe in it without drowning, while an elephant can swim in it."[13]

We might also wonder what innovative things he said, given his *Rule*'s ongoing, beyond-monasteries success. But Benedict did not seek to innovate. Instead, he consulted many traditional rules—by Basil, Pachomius, Augustine, John Cassian, the Italian *Rule of the Master*, and others—then made his *Rule* by "thin slicing," as Richard Rohr often calls it, referencing Malcolm Gladwell's popularization of the phrase for "sifting through the situation in front of us, throwing out all that is irrelevant while we zero in on what really matters."[14]

For example, where an earlier rule frequently referred to God as a terrifying Lord, Benedict emphasized God as a kind father, avoiding this anxious tone. He also dialed down their harsh asceticism and focused on a holistic way of embodied living, valuing equilibrium of soul and body to experience the "ineffable sweetness" of God's love.[15] To Benedict, it was important that his monks eat healthily, chant and sleep regularly, engage in physical work for about six hours a day, have daily set times for *lectio divina*, and even enjoy a summer siesta, if needed.

One of Benedict's most unobtrusive hospitable acts is that he wrote his *Rule* not in the erudite ancient classical Latin, nor in academic Latin, but in a more accessible Latin register. His brevity, simplicity, and kind tone drew his reader in completely.

In a hostile world where it might have seemed safer to buy a castle, pull up the drawbridge, and live behind thick stone walls, Benedict embraced poverty and lived out his Gospel-steeped Rule that teaches practicing hospitality toward the exiled stranger.

We remember too that *hostile*, *host*, and *hospitable* share a root meaning of "guest, chance comer, stranger." Benedict's life is a reminder, then, of the choice we face daily. *Is the stranger within me and outside of me treated as the honored guest or the hated enemy?* His life shows us that action and contemplation are the wise path of welcoming.

Luminous Darkness

By Mirabai Starr

THE DARK NIGHT OF PRISON

Juan de la Cruz, or St. John of the Cross (1542–1591), was twenty-nine years old and madly in love with God. The great living saint Teresa of Ávila (1515–1582) had spotted a sublime brilliance in this humble young friar and placed him in charge of her first reform convent.

Then, late one night, threatened by this movement to return the order to the contemplative path embodied by the Desert Fathers and Mothers, a contingent of mainstream Carmelites wrenched him from his bed and imprisoned him in their Toledo monastery.

His cell was a tiny closet that had formerly served as a latrine. There was not enough room to lie down, and the only window was far above his head. Through it, he could chart the course of three or four stars at a time as they passed slowly through space. Mostly, he sat very still in the darkness, clothed in the same thin garment he had been wearing when he was abducted, shivering through the cold months, sweltering in the heat.

Twice a day, the friars took him out and flogged him.

"Denounce Teresa!" they demanded. "Renounce the heresy of this so-called reform!"

But he would not betray the dream—the dream of a life of voluntary simplicity, solitude, and silence; a contemplative life based on the Gospel teachings of poverty of spirit and charity of heart; a life of stripping away rather than accumulating, of relinquishing power and seeking nothing, of nothing but loving friendship with the Divine and loving service to creation.

Little by little, into the darkness of his isolation, the love of God flowed.

When he was back in his cell after the floggings, the brothers would murmur theatrically outside his door.

"Did you hear?" one friar would hiss to another. "Teresa of Ávila has been arrested, and her followers have all abandoned her. The reform has collapsed."

They were lying.

Other times, they would mock the prisoner: "I guess your friends don't care about you after all, Father. Not a word from anyone. It appears that you have been entirely forgotten, as if you never existed at all."

More lies.

It was painful enough to be forgotten by the human beings he loved. But as the months ground by, he began to fear that he had also been abandoned by the Holy One. For the first time in his life, he questioned the existence of a God he could no longer feel or remember. And, as his soul dried up, he found he could not even conceive of this God to whom he had dedicated everything. Whenever he tried to pray, all he encountered was a cavernous emptiness.

Like the bride in the Song of Songs, he cried out, "Where have you hidden, my Beloved?"

Echoing from this cry came an outpouring of love poetry to God. His broken heart had become a garden in which the seeds of longing yielded a harvest of love-language. He committed each poem to memory and recited them all again and again until they were etched on his heart. His poems became simultaneously a call to and a response from his Beloved. Little by little, into the darkness of his isolation, the love of God flowed, illuminating his shattered heart and filling him with quiet joy.

At last, one dark night, a sympathetic guard turned the other way as the frail friar made his escape. Taking refuge among the sisters in a nearby convent, he fell into an ecstatic state from which he never recovered.

A FRIAR AND A HALF

EARLY IN THE sixteenth century, Gonzalo, a fair-skinned Spanish nobleman from a family of textile merchants, fell in love with Catalina, a North African weaver woman who had come to his door peddling cloth.

The Inquisition was at its pathological height. Purity of European blood was considered a sign of true devotion to the Church. Jews and Muslims, who had been living in Spain in relative harmony with Christians under Islamic rule for many centuries, collaborating on some of the greatest works of art, architecture, science, and mystical texts in the history of civilization, were being forced by the Roman Catholic Church to convert or be expelled from their homeland. Many *conversos*, caught in the act of practicing their ancestral faith, were exiled or executed.

For a wealthy Spaniard to marry a Moor required great courage, and Gonzalo's family disowned him as a result. This particular liaison was all the more risky in light of Gonzalo's own heritage: He probably came from a Jewish family, one that had successfully hidden its dangerous roots.

Juan de Yepes y Álvarez, who would one day be known as St. John of the Cross, was the child of this great love, and the cells of his body held the intermingled streams of Judaism and Islam.... Born in 1542 in the small village of Fontiveros, near the city of Ávila, John spent his early childhood wandering with his parents and his two older brothers in search of work. John's father, who apprenticed with his mother to learn the art of weaving, died of the plague when John was still a small boy. John's middle brother died of malnutrition soon after. Finally, his destitute mother settled what remained of her family in the market town of Medina del Campo.

When John was twelve, he found work at a local hospital, caring for patients with incurable diseases, including many with syphilis. John found deep purpose and even solace in tending the dying. He bathed their sores, listened to their stories, and sang them the Arabic ballads he had learned as a child. He collected food and funds for the hospital and dedicated his life to embracing the people whom society had abandoned.

Don Alonso, the hospital administrator, was impressed by the young man's intelligence and sensitivity. In hopes that John might become a priest and harness his gifts in service to the soul of humanity, Don Alonso paid for his education at a Jesuit college and later at the legendary University of Salamanca. After completing his studies at age twenty-one, John joined a community of Carmelite friars, where he took the name John of the Cross. He was inspired by the example of the early thirteenth-century Carmelites of the Holy Land, an order whose rule of life flowed from a vision of contemplative prayer and direct experience of the sacred. He was ordained as a priest in 1567.

But the sixteenth-century version of the Carmelite order had drifted far from its desert origins. Like other religious orders of the Roman Catholic Church, the Carmelites no longer placed primary emphasis on silence, stillness, and simplicity. Convents were endowed by the dowries of wealthy nuns who couldn't find husbands, while the monks competed for who could perform the most spectacular penances. Quickly disenchanted by performative religiosity, John was poised to leave the order and flee to the mountains to live as a holy hermit when a singular event changed the course of his life.

He met Teresa of Ávila.

Teresa, the mother abbess of a Carmelite monastery, was twice John's age, yet each instantly recognized the innate spiritual mastery in the other. Like John, Teresa longed for a return to the simple devotional life lived by their forebears at the foot of Mount Carmel. Teresa was actively engaged in reforming the order when she heard of this fiery friar who shared her yearning for a community based on the cultivation of silent prayer and an unmediated relationship with the Divine.

Malnourished by childhood poverty, John's growth had been stunted and, as a twenty-five-year-old man, he stood barely five feet tall. After her first thrilling encounter with him, Teresa declared that, while he might be small in stature, John of the Cross was great in

God. She referred to him as a "friar and a half" and declared him to be the father of her soul.... John of the Cross joined Teresa of Ávila's cause, and she immediately made him confessor to the nuns of her first convent.

John paid a high price for his devotion to Teresa and her reform movement. He was twenty-nine when he was abducted by the conventional Carmelite friars. After nine months of incarceration and torture, he ... spent the next two decades in dedicated service to the vision he shared with Teresa, returning the attention of the monks and nuns he guided to the radiant stillness of their own souls. He was happiest when he was most invisible, praying alone in the chapel of nature or addressing the spiritual yearnings of the nuns who adored him with humble lucidity.

Twenty years after his prison ordeal, John died of a recurring infection from the wounds he had sustained there. But during the period in between, he lived in ecstatic relationship to the Beloved. Love poetry flowed abundantly from his pen, and he radiated the bliss of perpetual intimacy with the Divine, touching everyone in his sphere with his deep quietude and playful wisdom.

THE DARKNESS THAT IS LIGHT

> Even though this holy night darkens the spirit,
> it does so only to light up everything.
> –St. John of the Cross, *Dark Night of the Soul*[1]

SOMETIMES IN THE spiritual life, if you are very lucky, the Holy One slams the door shut and plunges you into darkness.

This may occur when you are at your best, basking in the glow of tender feelings of devotion in prayer and practice–when, all at once, the ancient teachings of the masters make perfect sense.... People seem to be drawn toward your natural equanimity and inspiring way with words.

But then, suddenly, God bores you. Suddenly, you do not have any idea who this God even *is*.

Spiritual practice turns out to be more tedious than a teeth-cleaning, and just about as holy. Studying sacred literature feels like reading an economics textbook from the 1950s. Where not long ago you sat in the cathedral singing to God, tears of joy streaming down your face, now your heart has turned to clay, and you have stopped attending religious services. You used to be able to meditate for an hour and it felt like five minutes. Now you watch the clock as the minutes limp by and finally decide to get up off the cushion and go back to bed.

Finally empty, you are free to receive the Holy One.

What's happening here? You suspect that God is punishing you for all your carefully hidden faults, if God even exists at all, which is beginning to seem more and more unlikely. You resign yourself to abandonment. If you were God, you would give up on you, too, worthless wretch that you are.

You decide to confide in a couple of spiritual people you know. They smile knowingly and assure you that everyone grapples with periods of dryness and obscurity along the spiritual journey. They affirm your basic goodness and remind you that you are not so special that God would forsake you and nobody else. . . . Their words only make you feel worse. It's obvious that they have never felt what you are feeling and do not understand you at all.

You withdraw into yourself—which is exactly where God wants you. . . .

You stop fighting and, exhausted, rest in the darkness of unknowing. You have been drained and flattened. You sit in your brokenness and listen to the sound of your own breathing. There is nothing else to do. There is nowhere else to be.

Into this darkness of the soul, you eventually begin to notice a subtle inflowing of sweetness and ease. The ancient mystics call this surrender "infused contemplation." Finally empty, you are free to receive the Holy One. This new peace is not the fruit of an active practice of meditation. It is a fully receptive state. Your only task is simply to be. The Holy One will do all the rest.

The Beloved has purified you with fire–stripped away all attachments to how spiritual experience is supposed to feel and obliterated all mental constructs about what God is supposed to mean. He transmits his secret teachings of love, making you ready for union with him. Infused with his grace, you realize that what your old eyes mistook for darkness, your new eyes recognize as pure light.

Even though it impoverishes her, emptying her of
natural inclinations, it is only so that she will reach
out for the divine and freely enjoy the fruits of all
things, of above and of below.
　　　　–St. John of the Cross, Dark Night of the Soul[2]

Excerpt reprinted from Mirabai Starr, *Saint John of the Cross: Luminous Darkness* (Albuquerque, NM: CAC Publishing, 2022), 25–36. Reprinted with permission.

The Monastic Impulse Leads to Unintentional Menageries in Love

By Paul Swanson

A monk is one who is separated from all and united with all.
—Evagrius Ponticus[1]

> Monastic life is profoundly communitarian. The monastic community is rooted in *conversatio morum*, sharing in the things that really matter. In this *conversatio* the word is made flesh and expressed in a life-long commitment: the gift and gifting of self to and for others.... The human begins and ends with the search for the One—*monos* is a verb as well as a noun—a call as well as a description.
> —Brother John[2]

The word "monk" comes from the Greek word *monachos*, meaning "single" or "solitary." Hence I am massaging the phrase "monastic impulse" to imply an inborn desire to be single-minded in pursuit of the pearl of great price: God seen, revered, and participated in, in and through every thing.

In a combination of muddy loop-the-loops, I will attempt to unhinge the unseen incarnational monastic impulse from institutional life[3] so it can be seen as the instigator of flourishing in any alternative community of Christic refuge in times of exile. The singleness of this pursuit is what I am calling the monastic impulse here. The unfolding pathways of my days have led me to participate in a number of alternative communities, some for short stints and a few for long hauls. The monastic impulse is the primary inspiration for myself and others I know to congregate and contemplate around fires lit by the Beloved. In the broadest sense of the term, this is *conversatio morum*[4] on communities of refuge. In that spirit, I will focus on how *Sun House* (a masterful and profoundly mystical modern fictional tome by author David James Duncan) and the Beguines (a masterful and profound laywomen's Christian mystical movement of the thirteenth century) are in dialogue with my own lived experiences to vivify the multidimensional ways that alternative communities inspire, ripen, and animate transformation.

> Beguines encouraged fellow laypeople to follow their example and take responsibility for their own spiritual education.
> —Laura Swan, *The Wisdom of the Beguines*[5]

> I am nothing except Love.
> —Marguerite Porete, Beguine mystic[6]

As a student, I stumbled upon the Beguines twenty-five years ago and was slingshot over the moon with enthusiasm.[7] My monastic impulse was shocked by the images of their alternative communitarian life, mystical teaching, and poetry. With eyes and heart opened, I wanted to know more about this radical movement.

The Beguines' embodiment of God's love was not exhausted in service but further expressed in daring teachings, devotion, spiritual formation, and mystical poetry.

The Beguine movement was started in the thirteenth century by laywomen who lived outside the powers of their times by sharing resources, a common rule of life, and an entrepreneurial spirit in work and ministry. They enjoyed communal freedom by strategically employing an independent lifestyle as "a tool to work with the marginalized and the poor, in ways that they personally chose—and not under the direction and control of a bishop or nobleman. Their ministry was an expression of God's love for all, a love the Beguines sought to embody."[8] This embodiment and expression of God's love was at the center of Beguine life. This manifested in direct service to "the least of these": educating the poor, raising orphans, providing refuge for women marginalized by a patriarchal culture (for escaping bad marriages, resorting to sex work, having out-of-wedlock pregnancies, and evading societal pressures to marry), holding vigil amid hospice houses for the dying.[9]

When systems of power are souring life in the commons and at the margins, creative alternatives at the edges are needed, or life will spoil.

The Beguines' embodiment of God's love was not exhausted in service but further expressed in daring teachings, devotion, spiritual formation, and mystical poetry. Their preaching and teaching encouraged everyone to experience direct and intimate connection with God.[10] No clergy required. This was a revolutionary spirituality. For the Beguines, "prayer was being in the presence of God, seeking to unite their minds and hearts with the One they loved (and whom they frequently referred to as their 'Beloved.') A central goal in life for Beguines was unity of will–that their personal will would become so united with the will of God they essentially functioned as a unified whole."[11] This is the monastic impulse seeking to marry outward labor and service with inward devotion in daily life. As Hadewijch of Antwerp, my favorite Beguine poet, shared in a letter to another Beguine, "With the Humanity of God you must live here on earth, in the labors and sorrows of exile, while within your soul you love and rejoice for the truth of both the Humanity and the divinity is one single fruition."[12] This is the primacy of love in action in *this world*, as a dignified and dynamic unity of humanity and divinity.

As a younger man, I was dissuaded from studying the Beguines. They were easy to dismiss as heretics (though studies show most heresy charges against these independent preachers, healers, and mystics were politically motivated. Go figure).[13] I did not have the historical analysis at the time to recognize that when systems of power are souring life in the commons and at the margins, creative alternatives at the edges are needed, or life will spoil. It is in the commons, at the margins, and on the edges where the monastic impulse blooms.

> Since my early youth I have seen myself as a monk, but one without a monastery, or at least without walls other than those of the entire planet.
>
> —Raimundo Panikkar[14]

MY OWN MONASTIC impulse led me to the Center for Action and Contemplation in 2007. What drew me to the CAC was not Fr. Richard Rohr, but the CAC Eight Core Principles.[15] When I read the Eight Core Principles, they pierced me. They had a strong intuitive fidelity to the pearl of great price, orthopraxy with muscles, and no fixed end. My monastic impulse flared up. I wept, quit my job, and applied to be a work intern.[16]

My life was being stirred in a petri dish at a contemplative laboratory.

Although I lived in what seemed to be another country, 1500 miles from Albuquerque, I wanted a crack at living and working at a place that was bold enough to name these Core Principles. So, I became a CAC intern. We interns lived under one roof, worked necessary jobs, served at a local homeless shelter, tended the garden, and engaged in spiritual practice and formation together. My life was being stirred in a petri dish at a contemplative laboratory. The rapidity of growth under the tutelage of wonder, curiosity, and disciplined practice stunned me. My fellow interns and I came from different religious backgrounds, economic classes, seasons of life, and countries—it was a radical communal experiment with an expiration date. We knew when we arrived that we would leave one another. And we knew when we left that we had paid heed to what had pierced our lives and fanned the fire within.

> Wishing to teach fellow lay seekers a path to an intimate relationship with God, beguines first and foremost taught by example. They lived, to the best of their ability, what they preached. Even their critics, being uncomfortable with beguines teaching and preaching, begrudgingly acknowledged the good that the women accomplished.
> —Laura Swan, *The Wisdom of the Beguines*[17]

MY MATURING MONASTIC impulse led me to recognize the necessity of participation in community life—alternative communities that pursued radical gospel living in service to a living God. This led me to a Catholic Worker House, a Mennonite community, and a new monastic community.[18] Each was messy, beautiful, and with a cast of characters not of my choosing. Community is not a soft choice, for, as Benedictine Joan Chittister writes, "community itself is a spiritual act, a spiritual discipline, a spiritual force in society. No nonsense. No dishonesty. No posturing allowed. It is all a matter of being truly spiritual, truly dedicated to living a life of holiness, truly committed to a lifestyle that enriches life for us all.... It's a matter of what we really bring to the world, in and for the world community, that counts."[19] Life immersed in one community ultimately bubbles up and popples out to the shores of the world.

In 2023, a most curious novel came out: *Sun House* by David James Duncan. In *Sun House*, Duncan tells a sprawling story of what transformation of consciousness looks like and how it might be lived out in collective fidelity while valuing difference. The book is nearly 800 pages long, so forgive me for relaying only a few themes in broad strokes. The monastic impulse draws the characters of *Sun House* together, not into a commune, monastery, or intentional community– but into an *unintentional menagerie*. When Jamey Van Zandt, the character who coined the term "unintentional menagerie," was asked why he is hellbent on using that phrase for their shared life rather than "commune" or "intentional community," he responds,

> "It's important, no offense to anyone, because nearly all communes fail," Jamey said. "And strong human intentions are the main reason they do. *Intentionality* misses the mark as soon as it leads to *mental straining toward a fixed end*. Monsanto, the NRA, Ayn Rand's absurdly unimaginable fiction, Vatican edicts and so on, herd human lives into cold obedience to a manifesto with great *intentionality*, and look at the results. Sordid intention is so contagiously bad it's caused good intentions to become famous for paving the road to hell."

Good Lord, Jamey!" Ona burst out. "What's the antidote?"

"Paying heed to what *pierces* or tyrannizes it."[20]

THE INSPIRATION FOR this timely unintentional menagerie in *Sun House* was the Beguine movement. There are pages and pages that detail the vast wisdom and practical structure of this contemplative movement as a possible model for today. The unintentional menagerie in Sun House is called the Elkmoon Beguine & Cattle Company, which is a working cattle ranch that practices artistry in song and poem, Christic poverty and service, cottage industries, master craftmanship, healing work, land stewardship, and adept unpretentious spiritual formation in a non-cloistered community. It is revelatory to imagine the possibilities of what a committed band of pierced hearts can step into.

We must lean in and listen to what pierces our hearts, alone and together.

In *Sun House*, one of the silver-tongued elders of the unintentional menagerie (which they call E.B.&C. Co for short and themselves Elkmooners) says this on the wholeness of life they are attempting to live within: "We Elkmooners are a diverse crew in matters of the spirit, it's fair to say we each yearn, in our own idiosyncratic ways, for an inner and outer wholeness inseparable from Mother Earth's life and wholeness. And though we don't always like it, life on the E.B.&C. Co *forces* us to not just talk but to *walk* the largest possible fraction of that wholeness daily."[21] This indivisible yearning for wholeness is at the core of our being as planetwalkers in *this world*. This is the monastic impulse sputtering in pursuit of singleness of heart. Jesus calls this the pearl of great price. This is what draws together and sustains unintentional menageries in times of exile.

> You shall love the nothing. You shall flee the something.
> —Mechthild of Magdeburg, Beguine mystic[22]

> We must, without sparing, lose all for all.
> —Hadewijch of Antwerp, Beguine mystic[23]

> "I've heard you marvel at how, all day every day, the E.B.&C. Co throws the Industrial Suicide Machine into reverse and drives the opposite direction. It's true. But it's not accomplished by cult leaders and laws. We are *not* an intentional community. We are *not* an intentional community. We're an *unintentional menagerie*... joined not by didactic intent but by hearts pierced by unseen threads. It's an old, old magic. When even two such hearts align, things happen. Not easy things but, more often than not, *moving* ones."
> —Jamey Van Zandt, Elkmooner in *Sun House*[24]

THE TECHNOCRAT SAVIORS are flying to Mars to offer planetary offramps and schlupping digital diversions. They are scripting modern myths based on wealth and power that unthinkingly dismember, distract, and supplant the monastic impulse in the commons. What is the state of your monastic impulse? How are the bees of your attention filling the empty comb of the present? We must lean in and listen to what pierces our hearts, alone and together. My heart has been pierced by unseen threads. I go on to gaze upon the face of the Beloved in the work of my hands, my wife, my children, our neighbors, and even vitriolic politicos. The singleness of heart is pumping as both a verb and a noun in me. I stumble along within my unintentional menageries of belonging, seeking alternative directions.

My pierced heart is in the here and now, in *this world,* looking toward a Christian movement like the Beguines that births figures like Hadewijch, who faced "the reality of absence, exile, and despair for the sake of love" and willingly entered and lived within what she called "the deep, insurmountable darkness of love,"[23] a love that is shielded from systematization, exploitation, and fixed ends. A heart pierced by love is not pious, but awakened and revolutionary.

May your monastic impulse guide you into an unintentional menagerie that humbly sings a radical song of loving service together, in a quivering, yet unwavering transformative harmony that concomitantly unfolds into God's restoring justice. This is the song of Oneness that the Beloved longs to hear us sing.

Listen

By Barbara C. Otero-López

Despiertate mija—Wake up, my child. These words are echoing in my dreams of late. In my mind's eye, I hear my mother's whisper, urging me to wake up—my wise and resilient mother who has joined the ancestors and speaks to me from the other side. When I listen closely, I hear her voice joined by others: *Levantate mija—Stand up, my child.* This call is comforting and insistent at the same time. I am being called to *listen*. There is a story stirring inside of me that wants to be told.

    I think I've been hearing this call all my life, but the voices haven't always been so clear. When my mother was alive, I think they were speaking *through* her. As she was teaching me, she was their translator. She translated their wisdom through all the ways she taught me to love: the way she lived with laughter and joy each day of her life, despite the sorrow she felt and held so tenderly.

    My mother lived a difficult life, but no one would have known. She carried her pain in silence, like the women in her family who came before her. She taught me and my daughters how to transform tears and sorrow into tastes and smells, songs and laughter. I can still hear her rolling pin clanking rhythmically as she rolled out tortillas with skill and ease. She passed on acceptance as she taught me, and my daughters after me, that it was okay that our tortillas didn't come out so round. As a little girl, I would stand on a chair next to my mother, her with her big rolling pin and me with my small one, rolling out tortilla after tortilla. I remember that, more times than most, she had tears in her eyes and, as she rolled, her tears fell and mixed into the dough. I didn't know why she was crying so silently, so stoically. I just remember thinking that it was the salt in her tears that made her tortillas the best I ever tasted. I suppose in my heart I did know why she was crying. I did bear witness to some of her pain. But what I remember most was not those hard times in my home as a child, but the way my mother did all she could to shield me and my brother from it and how she carried it with resilience and grace.

It was the salt in her tears that made her tortillas the best I ever tasted.

My mother exemplified joy and love, and I am sure this way of life for her was not by accident. This was something she herself witnessed and learned from her mother, and I'm guessing that my grandmother learned from her mother before her. Both my grandmothers translated in their own way the wisdom of their ancestors. I live the memories of my grandmothers teaching me how to make flavors come to life through posole, biscochitos, sopapillas, and tamales and how to combine the three sisters—beans, squash, and corn—to make calabacitas. Love and resilience live on so strongly through food in my family.

My mother and grandmothers also taught me the healing powers of herbs: *yerba buena*—mint, the herb which can relieve the sourness in life; the cleansing power of sage that smells so beautifully earthy and grows abundantly in the *llano*—the New Mexican countryside; *oshá* and *yerba mansa*—plants whose roots are used as *remedios* to soothe and heal any number of illnesses. For my mother and my grandmothers, plants had a spirit and thus deserved love and respect. I learned from them that by combining respect for nature's healing plants and a deep love for others, alchemy happens through teas and tinctures to bring forth healing and antidotes for ailments of all kinds.

Then there are the songs, the music that echoes over time. One grandmother lives in my memory as a woman who worked very hard and cared deeply for others, and her work was often accompanied by song:

Espíritu Santo ven, ven;
Espíritu Santo ven, ven;
Espíritu Santo ven, ven, en el nombre del Señor.
Acompáñame, ilumíname, toma mi vida.
Santifícame y transfórmame.
Espíritu Santo ven, ven.

Come Holy Spirit come;
Come Holy Spirit come;
Come Holy Spirit come, in the holy name of God.
Walk with me, enlighten me, you have my life.
Bless me and transform me.
Come Holy Spirit come.

These are stories I know. These are stories I have lived and witnessed. These are stories that have been translated to me. But what of those stories of my ancestors that live silently within me, that don't want to be lost or forgotten? These stories are calling me to listen, to wake up so I too may become a translator of their wisdom.

The stories that live inside me are rooted in the history, traditions, and culture of my home in New Mexico. Dr. Barbara Holmes (Dr. B; 1943–2024) taught the importance of learning about our roots "because place matters, because geographies can be sacred. They hold memories. There are thin places where mystery abides still to this day. Like a sacred geologist, if you know where you are from and you know who your people are, then you know the stories and the mythologies and the connections. You'll find your way to mystery."[1]

Through her teachings, Dr. B has given me the language and permission to become a sacred geologist. Throughout my life, I have been becoming my own version of a sacred geologist, always fascinated and haunted by my own sense of place. Early in my childhood, my strong sense of place felt stifling, more like a trap that I needed to escape. I am deeply rooted here in my New Mexican home. My Spanish ancestors settled here in the early 1600s, and my Pueblo ancestors have cared for this land longer than I can trace through any family tree. There is beauty and richness in the culture of my ancestors, and there is also a lot of pain and trauma that lives in my DNA and has been passed down over generations.

I think, as a child, it was this trauma that I sensed the most. There was an indescribable sadness that whispered in the breeze out in the *llano*, that sang alongside us in the pews at church, and that sat with us, listening to our stories at the kitchen table. I think now that it was this deep sadness that made me feel helpless and trapped. I would hear stories about my Indigenous ancestors who were *Genízaros*–Indigenous indentured servants to wealthy Spanish families. But those stories were told in whispers, not to be shared outside of the family for fear of shame or being thought less-than by others. It was no wonder that being born with light skin or light eyes in my family was thought to be a blessing of God. This meant that our Indigenous secret might just be lost or forgotten. I was born with light skin and light eyes, but this never felt like a blessing. It only made me feel different, as if, in some way, I was living a lie with my very existence.

What of those stories of my ancestors that live silently within me, that don't want to be lost or forgotten?

As an adult, I took any opportunity I could to escape the trap which was my geographical home. I traveled and lived in several different places. Becoming a sacred geologist, I always wanted to seek to understand those who were rooted in those places, to learn about the history, culture, and stories that lived on in those places. When I lived in other places, it became my practice to learn how to forge right relationship with the land and those who called it home. It was through this practice and appreciation for the beauty and trauma which is rooted in all the places I have lived, that I sought to return to the source of what made me feel so trapped and stifled, to return to and embrace my geographical home and learn more deeply about my own history.

As in so many places across the United States and around the world, Indigenous men, women, and children in New Mexico have suffered a great deal of trauma, generationally and historically. My ancestral family includes many Indigenous women who were taken captive by Spanish conquistadors and settlers. These women were captured and taken from their own families into communities that were vastly different from their own. They were taken as captives, wives and slaves. They were used as bartering tools and to secure alliances.[2] They were exiled from the lives they once knew and were forced to live as wives and slaves. These women bore the trauma of captivity, the trauma of exile in the land of their own people. They were forced to marry and bear the children of their captors. Trauma such as this is known to be passed on through the womb, through the umbilical cord, from mother to child, and then again to that child's child.[3] *Sustos* is a Spanish word that names soul wounds such as these.

Despite the pain and trauma of captivity and forced assimilation into a culture and society which was not their own, despite their *sustos*, these women learned how to love and pass on this love through food, song, healing, tradition, and the love of God and all Her creation. This love in the time of exile was a sacred love, one borne of resilience and silent resistance. And, as I have learned, just as trauma and soul wounds are passed on to successive generations through DNA, love and resilience are too.

As Dr. B has taught us, "You journey with your ancestors. That's why knowing your roots is important, because whether you know it or not, they're journeying with you. Wouldn't you want the help? Wouldn't you want the warnings? Wouldn't you want the blessings of those who have gone before you?"[4]

I will never know the detailed stories of these women whom I call grandmothers. I may not know their birth names or where exactly their people were rooted and cared for the land, but I do know their resilience, and I know their love. Their love and resilience will live on through the food, songs, and *remedios* that my mother and my grandmothers shared with me. Their *sustos* will forever live on through my tears and through my stories that I share with my family. The presence of my ancestors is not only a comfort. They are also still teaching me, and I have so much yet to learn.

I am going to be a grandmother myself now, and I can hear my mother and my grandmothers calling me to *listen* and to *wake up* and live the stories they want me to pass on, to continue the honor of being the translator of memories and mythologies, to pass on the love and resilience which has been passed on to me.

I hope I am also learning what it means for me to *stand up* in loving protest and how to model what this could look like in my family. Society pressures us to overwork and think we can do and "have it all," whatever "having it all" means. We are anxious about what our future holds while at the same time feeling overwhelmed about the complexities of our present lives. Maybe, the lessons I have learned about loving protest and resilience can help me to pass on how to listen to the pain and symptoms our bodies are feeling and not live in chronic sacrifice, pushing ourselves beyond our limits to disease and exhaustion. Maybe, I can help to pass on a culture of healthy boundary-setting while also showing up with love.

> I can hear my mother and my grandmothers calling me to *listen* and to *wake up*.

There is an invitation for us all in times such as these. We are all being called to *wake up* and name our sadness, pain, and trauma, to allow our tears to flow and season our very lives. Times such as these are also calling us to *stand up*, to avoid becoming cynical and bitter, and to not be consumed and overpowered by our anger and sadness. Instead, we are to transform all that into something much more generative. We have much to learn from our ancestors, from their stories of trauma and from their loving protest of resilience.

I believe that in times such as these, we are all being called to *listen*. What stories are your ancestors wanting to tell through you?

My Exile Trilogy

By Pamela Ayo Yetunde

PART I: MATERNAL AND FAMILIAL EXILE

I lived and survived most of my early life as a popular person because I learned to be a likeable and pleasing daughter and friend. My mother taught me how to be the best of friends to others. I witnessed her delighting in relationships. My mother was also my best friend. Our bond grew closer every year after I dedicated myself to her well-being when her husband of ten years, my father, died suddenly when my mom was just thirty-three years old.

I especially enjoyed accompanying my mom on her spontaneous weekend "popcorn calls." Never once did I experience anyone not being happy to see us. When I was a child, I gushed when people said I was just like her.

Yet, in retrospect, we were always at risk of being exiled from one another.

My mother, born in 1937 in a small rural town in Arkansas and raised in Gary, Indiana in a Black United Methodist family, was the first person who introduced me to a white transgender woman, her work colleague at an army base in Indianapolis, Indiana, in 1982. It was my mom who told me that Tina (not her real name) deserved as much respect as anyone else. I believed her because she was absolutely grounded in her Christian faith of radical non-discriminatory love and lived that out through her friendships.

My greatest legacy from my mother is her lesson in friendship. Other blessings have come from the narratives shared by my pastoral counseling clients about what it took to live and survive their lives. Combining my family narrative with theirs (and some research for good measure), I have come to believe that there comes a time in a person's life when we make a conscious decision to risk being exiled by the ones we love. Even my mother, the radically non-discriminatory loving person in solidarity with Tina, sent me into exile when I told her that I, her "mini me" extension, was gay. It was the most painful relational experience I have ever had.

Fortunately, I was living in San Francisco when I came out (the second time) and attending Glide Memorial United Methodist Church, led by the Rev. Cecil Williams (1929–2024) and his wife, poet Jan Mirikitani (1941–2021).

PART II. HEALING THROUGH EXILE IN PLACES OF EXILES

I ENTERED GLIDE WITH an exile consciousness. I grew up in the United Methodist Church, yet I initially attended Glide by sitting in the back of the church, as close to the exit as possible. I didn't want to be seen and especially didn't want to be heard sobbing. I didn't want to subject myself to concern and care. I didn't want to shake hands or be hugged with compassion. I didn't want to talk about my pain, loneliness, and doubt. Why was I there, if I did not want human interaction? Looking back, I realize I needed an affirming spiritual home, but I wasn't sure I knew anymore how to live and worship amongst United Methodists.

In short order, I learned that I was an exile among exiles. Cecil and Jan talked about the many ways they had been exiled for their liberation theologies, interracial relationship, and radically inclusive ministry. Glide was in the Tenderloin neighborhood of exiles, a neighborhood I chose to live in, and as I grew into the awareness that I was in a swirling vortex of exiles, I began to move from the back of the church to near the middle, to join the LGBTQIA+ affinity group, and to share my exile story within the group.

There comes a time in a person's life when we make a conscious decision to risk being exiled by the ones we love.

At one of our meetings, weeks before the storied San Francisco Pride Parade was to take place, one of the group's members suggested I read, during church service, the hate-filled, violent, and vulgar letter my mother wrote to me after I came out. You see, my master teacher in how to be a great friend, even to transgender people in Indianapolis, Indiana in 1982, accused me, her extension, of child molestation! That accusation was about the closest thing I had ever experienced to being stabbed in the heart. Still, I thought my affinity group members had made an inappropriate request. Loving my mother still, I asked why they thought I would betray my mother in front of hundreds of people. Did they think I would do that just because she had turned her back on me, because she had wounded me in the worst possible ways? I initially refused to expose my mother's private communication, but they convinced me that reading the letter, in all its vileness, would be liberatory for people to hear on Gay Pride Sunday.

Now, I had another risky decision to make on my exile journey. Would I go from the back of the church, where my silent screams of family exile were expressed in sobs, to the front of the stage, where there would be no hiding place? On that Gay Pride Sunday, at that liberation theology church called Glide, in the Tenderloin–in the vortex of exiles–I got on stage and Rev. Cecil handed me the mic. I'll return to what happened later.

PART III. WORKING WITH INTERNATIONAL EXILES

I BECAME AN ASYLUM Officer with the Immigration and Naturalization Service (INS) just before coming out and as I began attending Glide. Asylum Officers were responsible for interviewing people in exile who had left their countries because they were pushed out, threatened with physical harm or death if they stayed, and who would face persecution if they were deported to their country of origin. They were seeking safe harbor from persecution in San Francisco. So was I. Why was I doing this work when I needed to work on myself?

In 1984, I visited a refugee camp in Zimbabwe. That experience of witnessing mass suffering left an indelible impression in and on every part of my being. I don't recall ever seeing a homeless person while growing up in Indianapolis, nor did we talk at home about war. I don't recall seeing coverage of wars in Africa on TV or reading about these wars in the newspaper. To come face to face with thousands of homeless people living under makeshift tarp-covered structures, with seemingly nothing on their backs but threadbare materials, was a traumatic but necessary wound to my naïve religious beliefs.

> "What is your responsibility, as a friend to those seeking safety, in the net/work at this time?"

I returned from Zimbabwe to Indianapolis with the vow that I would never embrace ignorance of the world. I moved to the Netherlands for two years as a Brethren Volunteer Service (BVS) volunteer and worked on nuclear disarmament and human rights abuses in Eastern Europe. I also traveled extensively during that time. In 1988, I was a BVS volunteer with the Washington Office on Africa in DC, working on anti-apartheid activism. Then, in 1989 I went to law school with an interest in advocating for human rights. I took courses in international and immigration law with the hope of becoming an effective human rights advocate.

When the opportunity to become an Asylum Officer presented itself in 1991, I applied, having a deeper understanding of what it meant for me and others to be exiled.

Given the 2024 reelection of an avowed xenophobic, anti-nonwhite and anti-immigrant president who ran on a xenophobic and nationalistic agenda, it is important to note that the US is not a signatory to the 1951 Convention that defines what a refugee is, but it is a party to the 1967 Protocol which broadens the regions where a refugee can flee from. It is not likely the US will continue its signatory status with the promise–or threat–of mass deportations looming. Thousands of those who have found refuge here are likely to be exiled again–and into places where they are likely to be harmed or killed.

CONCLUSION

When I recall the stories of my exiles and the exiles of asylum seekers, I cannot think of one person I know whom I would want to experience being forced to be on the run. Yet, to be ostracized by my mother, who was my best friend and who taught me how to be a friend; to have my religious beliefs shattered in Zimbabwe; to be in a neighborhood, city, and church of exiles as I interviewed political exiles, I know I wouldn't be the person and pastoral counselor that I am without having had these experiences. I also hold the humbling reality of being caught in Indra's Net, the inescapable network of our mutuality, as Dr. Martin Luther King Jr. (1929–1968) called it. This knowledge causes me to ask myself, "What is your responsibility, as a friend to those seeking safety, in the net/work at this time?"

Asking ourselves moral questions aids our ethical development and judgment. Two days after Donald Trump was reelected as president of the US, a federal judge struck down President Biden's attempt to protect from deportation undocumented immigrants married to US citizens. Is this the beginning of the bloodbath Trump promised? If children were taken from parents and put in cages as their parents were deported, we can expect that immigrant spouses will be separated from the citizens they're married to.

It is very humbling, ideal-shattering, and morally injurious when we learn that we are part of a system that is causing exile through various acts, including immigration policies. Can my mother's lessons in friendship, my experience in family exile, what I know about healing in spiritual community, and the strategy of scapegoating immigrants of color teach us something about the deep, existential morass of suffering that we keep digging deeper? Yes. It is possible to love while in exile. I loved my mother while I was in exile, and I learned about loving the refugee when I visited the camp in Zimbabwe. I saw how those in exile can love those in exile. I learned that there are ways for countries to support asylum seekers, but we cannot intentionally exile others, call it love, and be people of integrity.

We cannot welcome exiles and then, upon their entry, re-brutalize them. We need to return to valuing civility, and this can be done when we understand the value of friendship, the pain of exile, and the necessity of spiritual friends. We would do well to return to respecting the rule of law promulgated by democratic systems geared toward human flourishing. We can appreciate and protect the rule of law when we understand the purpose of the US Constitution, and we can value and protect the US Constitution when we understand the necessity of individual freedom and responsibility.

Can love and wisdom flourish between exiled people? Absolutely. My mother, at the time of this writing, is still alive and has been in my care for ten years. I knew at a young age that it was probable that she would need me in her old age and that I would want to be there for her. My immense gratitude to her for giving me life and sustaining me in the years when I needed it most have helped me abide, with love for her, even when she hated me and sent me into exile.

When I recall her expressions of rage and exile, I recall the letter she wrote to me that I was prepared to read at Glide on that Pride Sunday. As I approached the stage with letter in hand, about to engage in a liberatory act on behalf of the congregation by invading my mother's privacy, my letter-holding hand was shaking so much that congregants could hear the rustling of the papers through the microphone. My anxiety was amplified throughout the large sanctuary, before 500 people, and I was sweating bullets.

To ease my nerves, Rev. Cecil approached me, gently took the letter out of my hand, and said, "Speak from your heart." I trusted him and his intervention, but I felt that I didn't have time to really locate my deepest intentions. I didn't really trust that my speech would reflect the intensity and truth of my pain and my love. In angst, I blurted out words. I don't remember what I said, because I spoke in a moment of dissociation, but I do remember the standing ovation.

Even in exile, in a city of exiles, in a church of exiles, led by leaders in exile, while working with people in exile who were seeking safety, I know that being in exile is painful, but it doesn't prevent the presence of love. I also know that the wisdom produced by the pain of exile, coupled with love, must be put into action to reduce human rights abuses when intentional exile becomes part of public policies.

In these times of great personal and global migration and strife, may we find our way forward to home, through friendship, in the wisdom that comes from reflecting on the pain of being in exile, the compassion that comes when we witness mass suffering, and the love that endures through deep gratitude.

Letter to the Parts of Me I Have Tried to Exile

By Rosemerry Wahtola Trommer

I'm sorry. I thought banishing you
was the way to become better,
more perfect, more good, more free.
The irony: I thought if I cut you off
and cast you out, if I built the walls
high enough, then the parts left would be
more whole. As if the sweet orange
doesn't need the toughened rind,
the bitter seed. As if the forest

doesn't need the blue fury of fire.
It didn't work, did it, the exile?
You were always here, jangling
the hinges, banging at the door,
whispering through the cracks.
Left to myself, I wouldn't have known
to take down the walls,
nor would I have had the strength to do so.
That act was grace disguised as disaster.
But now that the walls are rubble,
it is also grace that teaches me to want
to embrace you, grace that guides me
to be gentle, even with the part of me
that would still try to exile any other part.
It is grace that invites me
to name all parts beloved.
How honest it all is. How human.
I promise to keep learning how
to know you as my own, to practice
opening to what at first feels unwanted,
meet it with understanding,
trust all belongs, welcome you home.[1]

The Countercultural Spirituality of the Desert Christians

By Belden Lane

The threat of desert landscape—from its grudging stinginess with water to its poisonous lizards and waiting vultures—has a way of eliciting the sharp, lean qualities of attentiveness and indifference. Both are desert virtues, honed by exposure to the elements. The one is necessary for survival. No one lasts in the desert without constant attentiveness to exterior and interior landscapes alike. One must keep an eye out for landmarks, the position of the sun in the sky, tracks in the sand, threatening clouds. But equally important is staying attuned to one's inner condition—the progress of fatigue, the irritation of blisters, the forgetfulness to which the mind is prone, the slow rise of panic at the fear of being lost. The desert fathers and mothers spoke of this attentiveness as *agrupnia*, the spiritual discipline of "wakefulness."[1]

The other virtue of "indifference" is the more slowly learned attitude of abandonment that grows from prolonged desert experience.[2] It means learning to ignore the things that are not important, being able–as one prepares for desert travel–to know what to leave behind. It, too, is directed toward interior as well as exterior landscapes. One must learn to accept the empty silence, to ignore sun and heat, to be untroubled by the scarcity of food–by the sparseness of everything other than space. Yet even more important, this indifference must be aimed inwardly at the self. It means not taking the ego too seriously, being able to watch one's compulsive needs wilt under the discipline of inattention. The desert invites an ignoring of the ego, its separation from the inner audience to which it continually plays for sympathy and admiration. The desert fathers and mothers spoke of this indifference as *apatheia*, the spiritual discipline of "detachment" or "dispassion," the practice of apathy with respect to matters of unimportance....

True indifference is rooted in a very conscious caring.

Attentiveness and indifference are, respectively, the constructive and deconstructive poles of the spiritual life. They tell us when to pay attention and when to let go, what to concentrate on and what to ignore, how to survive and how to abandon everything that is not necessary. T.S. Eliot, in his poem "Ash Wednesday," prayed for both: "Teach us to care and not to care."[3] John Climacus, the crusty old abbot of the monastery of Mount Sinai, understood these virtues as two of the most important rungs of his *Ladder of Divine Ascent*.[4]

They stand in paradoxical relation to each other, these two disciplines of the spirit: how to pay attention and how not to pay attention (and when to apply which of the two standards). Nothing else is more important or more difficult in one's faltering practice of a life of prayer....

For the early fathers and mothers, the immensity of the desert's indifference, suggesting for them the even greater immensity of God, offered great clarity about what did and did not matter, about what they would attend to and what they would ignore. In the calm, critical judgment of divine insouciance, bold decisions could be made about how the community of faith would conduct itself in the world.

To use the provocative language of Stanley Hauerwas and William Willimon, the desert Christians understood the church as an alien community no longer caught up in the anxious, self-interested preservation of the world-as-it-is. Their practice of indifference to the dominant social values of their age, exercised from the desert's edge, stood in stark contrast to the accommodating spirit of post-Constantinian, urban Christianity. Indeed, they understood their "oddness" to be an essential part of their faithfulness to Christ and the new community being formed in their midst.[5]

The indifference practiced by this desert colony of believers took shape in response to the social and political preoccupations of a compulsive world. In their reading of the gospel, they knew that a person's worth could never be measured by reference to any contemporary cult of success. The esteem with which they were held by others remained a matter of utter inconsequence.[6] They came to regard glib praise as swift cause for distrust. When an angel of light appeared to one of the brothers, saying, "I am Gabriel and I've been sent to you [above all the other monks]," the brother knew immediately that it was the devil. He replied with artless candor, "I'm sorry. There must be some mistake. Gabriel would never appear to the likes of me."[7]

Becoming equally indifferent to the praise and blame of the world was one of the primary goals of spiritual discipline in the desert. Learning not to care was a matter of utmost importance. Yet the desert masters were careful to distinguish between "true" and "false" indifference. True indifference was the fruit of contemplation, a direct result of disciplined attentiveness. The "no" of desert *apatheia* could emerge only out of deep certainty about the "yes" of the gospel. Detachment from the world and its values required informed, deliberate choices about what does and does not matter in light of Jesus and the inbreaking of his kingdom. True indifference is rooted in a very conscious caring.

False indifference, by contrast, was seen as an easy, casual matter of choosing haphazardly by neglect. It dissolved very readily into the world of the seven deadly sins—sloth or *accidie*, the lazy sullenness and despairing indiscipline of not caring about anything. Maurice Sendak whimsically satirizes this vice in his tiny cautionary tale for children entitled *Pierre*. There the constant refrain of his young protagonist is "I don't care." All threats are empty, all promises void for children like Pierre who live beyond hope. In the desert experience of the early Christians, such was the temptation of despair that often struck at noon, with the sun high overhead, the heat oppressive, mind and body giving in to the weary, monotonous passing of time.

> To cease to be driven by the fear of what other people think is to become a threat to the world as we know it.

False indifference is the scourge of domesticated Christianity, tired and worn out, readily accommodating itself to its culture, bowing to the social pressures of the status quo. It remains so tame as to fear nothing so much as the disdain of sophisticated unbelief. This is the indifference that allows the church to abandon its call to radical obedience to Christ in the world. It becomes the driving force behind every injustice, allowing dominant cultural forms to remain unchallenged by people too indifferent to care.

But indifference properly understood can become a source of profoundly liberating power. Adopted as a discipline of ignoring what is not important, in light of the truth of the gospel, it becomes a countercultural influence of great significance. People who pay attention to what matters most in their lives, and who learn to ignore everything else, assume a freedom that is highly creative as well as potentially dangerous in contemporary society. Having abandoned everything of insignificance, they have nothing to lose. Apart from being faithful to their God, they no longer care what happens to them.[8]

Were Christians (and others) to practice this stubborn desert discipline today, they would find a freedom that is refreshing and contagious to some, but also threatening and intolerable to others. Unjust societal structures and people addicted to power will not tolerate being ignored. They are profoundly threatened by those not subject to their influence, those no longer playing by the accepted rules. To cease to be driven by the fear of what other people think is to become a threat to the world as we know it. Only at great personal risk does one become indifferent to the accepted standards and expectations of the dominant culture.

Yet the people willing to assume this risk, the ones who find the center of their existence outside the cultural milieu, are those who model for us today the vitality of Christian faith....

This marriage of attentiveness and indifference gives birth at last to desert love. Such is the inevitable fruit of *agrupnia* and *apatheia*, the flowering of *agape*. Evagrius affirmed this from his fourth-century habitat in the desert west of the Nile when he claimed that desert *apatheia* has a daughter whose name is love. She is a full-blooded and lovely child, this one, a desert gift awakened by attentiveness and purified through the long exercise of holy indifference.

Longing for God is the highest desire to which the desert gives birth.

It was love more than anything else that drew the Egyptian fathers and mothers to the trackless desert beyond the Nile. They knew that scarcity and dry land awaken desire. Longing is the first product of desert experience. In the heat of the Egyptian sun, love bursts into flame as desire and is banked by the discipline into a slow and steady burn....

The desert Christians were fully aware of this propensity of a dry and thirsty land to stir the human passions. Accounts of their lives are filled with temptation narratives. Far from being a place of escape and freedom from conflict, the desert became a battleground. They recognized how the mind reaches distractedly for everything they had abandoned at the desert's edge. Their sense sharpened by the desert's minimalist vision, they recall in exquisite detail the loveliness of all they had relinquished in coming. The desert makes it easy to yield to the seduction of the mirage, building cities of memory on the sands of nothing....

Longing for God is the highest desire to which the desert gives birth. "Lucky the man," wrote John Climacus from his monastery at Sinai, "who loves and longs for God as a smitten lover does for his beloved."[9] This is the desire of a "stag, enflamed by love, as if struck by an arrow." It is the "inebriation of the soul."[10] Only in the desert is such longing made perfect. Brought to careful focus by the exercise of attentiveness and winnowed by indifference, the monk becomes a lover of God *par excellence*.

But how does this happen? If the desert, in its bleak emptiness, gives rise to frenzied desire, how is this desire made pure, stripped of its illusions, and reconsecrated as love? If wild terrain initially evokes a nervous attentiveness, rooted in one's anxious need for survival, how is this attentiveness slowly transformed into the calm and undistracted watchfulness of the desert saints? The answer, as Evagrius knew, lies in the exercise of *apatheia* as the mother of *agape*. Indifference, aimed at one's exercise of desert attentiveness, turns frantic desire into focused love.

The early desert fathers and mothers accomplished this task by incorporating into their discipline the very qualities of simplicity and redundancy that characterized their environment. Attending over and over to the same repetitive detail with unblinking watchfulness became the highest aim of desert prayer. Only as one's attention was narrowly focused–by means of a simple, repetitive prayer, by the monotonous motion of the hands in weaving–could one learn gradually to be fully present, without distraction, in any given moment to whatever presents itself. This, and this only, is the final meaning of love.

Reprinted from Belden Lane, *The Solace of Fierce Landscapes: Exploring Desert and Mountain Spirituality* (Oxford University Press, 1998), 188–189, 192–193, 196–197, 199–200. Reprinted with permission from Oxford University Press.

The Holy Longing

By Connie Zweig

In every mystical tradition, saints and lovers speak eloquently of the soul's search for the beloved, its yearning for the gods, its longing for communion. The bride in the Hebrew *Song of Solomon* sings her erotic yearning for her bridegroom, desiring to kiss him because his love is better than wine. The bride proclaims fervent union at last: "My beloved is mine and I am his" (2:16).

The Greek *maenads*, or madwomen, dressed in fawn skins and ivy crowns, carried lit torches and danced wildly around Dionysus, desiring nothing but union with him. The Egyptian divine queen, Isis, lamented and longed for her murdered husband, Osiris. After finding his body parts and rejoining them, she united with him. Osiris was resurrected a god, king of the dead. In the Hindu tradition of devotion, milkmaids, known as *gopis*, long for union with Krishna, the dark blue god. Krishna's sixteenth-century devotee Mirabai wanted to be turned into a heap of incense, burned into ash, and smeared on Krishna's chest.

I wonder why the metaphor of burning recurs again and again in the words of mystics, saints, and devotional poets in their attempts to describe the ardor of human-divine love. St. John of the Cross (1542–1591) said he was fired by love's urgent longings for Christ, the divine beloved. Jewish mystics declare that burning ecstasy unlocks the meaning of life. If we fulfill the commandments but don't feel the burning, they say, we won't feel the burning in paradise either. Rumi, the thirteenth-century Sufi poet (1207–1273), declared that a burning of the heart is more precious than everything else because it calls god secretly in the dark.

More recently, eminent psychologist Carl Jung (1875–1961) proclaimed in *The Psychology of Kundalini Yoga*: "A man who is not on fire is nothing; he is ridiculous, he is two-dimensional. He must be on fire even if he does make a fool of himself. A flame must burn somewhere, otherwise no light shines; there is no warmth, nothing."[1]...

I suggest that it is because of this holy longing for something Other, this timeless yearning for union with something beyond ourselves, that human beings sit still, cross-legged, eyes closed, as the splendors of spring pass us by. It is because of this longing that we strive to lose ourselves in one another in ecstatic embrace, like Shiva and Shakti weaving creation. It is because of this longing that we build Sistine Chapels, sculpt the David, and compose the Messiah. It is even because of it that we search intensively for the smallest bit of matter, the "god particle," which might be the ultimate building block of life.

It is also because of this holy longing that Islamic fundamentalists fighting a *jihad*, or holy war, eagerly sacrifice their lives to go to paradise. It is because of this longing that cult fanatics, such as those at Jamestown, commit group suicide to attain the other world. It is because of this longing that monks and nuns wall off the difficult demands of bodily life and bury their emotional wisdom like hidden treasure. It is because of this longing that faithful churchgoers and aspiring meditators refuse to see what appears before them as spiritual abuse, perpetrated in the name of god....

AWAKENING TO HOLY LONGING

A FAMOUS JEWISH MYSTIC, Rabbi Abraham Kook (1865–1935), pointed out that the person who tries to sustain themselves only from the surface of life will suffer terrible impoverishment. "Then he will feel welling up within himself a burning thirst for that inner substance and vision which transcends the obvious surfaces. From such inner sources he will seek the waters of joy which can quicken the dry outer skeleton of life."[2]

This innate burning thirst can be felt in many ways. For some, the holy longing can be detected as a nagging awareness of a lack or a fleeting sense of something more. At the age of fifty, one client sat across from me with a challenging glare: "I feel a constant, gnawing ache inside. Time is passing. I know this is not all there is."

Her statement implied unspoken questions begging for answers. I recalled Jung declaring that every patient he saw over the age of thirty-five was suffering from a religious problem. My client's pressing desire for something more pointed to her unconscious need for meaning and value, a need that was essentially religious because it revolved around her relation to larger forces, higher powers, or what we may call the gods.

Early childhood experiences of abuse, grief, and loss lead many people to seek relief from suffering, but more as well: Caught in feelings of anger and bitterness, they seek compassion and forgiveness. Trapped in feelings of isolation, they seek communion. Entering therapy to minister to past wounds, they begin to ask spiritual questions of meaning and depth. The pain that had seemed so purposeless and arbitrary is the very thing that sets them on the path.

Other people hear what mystics refer to as the still, quiet voice, or what the Sufis refer to as the call of the beloved. After that, they intuit that this world of the senses is not all there is. They wander restlessly from place to place, relationship to relationship, church to church, guru to guru. Their relentless hunger drives them here and there, but the smorgasbord of tastes never satisfies.

Many people experience their longing as a yearning for romantic love. Their hunger for the ideal loved one compels them to place relationship on the altar, above all other things. And, believing in the sacred power of love to heal them, even to save them, they anoint the lover with special gifts and unknowingly ask him or her to stand in for the divine.

Some women long for a divine child to redeem them. I have met women who, since their own youth, have yearned for the birth of a special child whose unconditional love will reward them. Or, disillusioned with a romantic beloved, a parent may unconsciously channel holy longing toward an innocent child, who becomes the family savior.

Others set their longing in a spiritual framework and feel it as a yearning for the light, which compels them to purify themselves of darkness. They may attempt to achieve this through strict diets and fasting or yoga and meditation. They may seek a teacher who is ahead of them on the path and who can relieve them of sins through practice or good deeds. They may imagine their objective as a desired shift in consciousness, which offers an end to isolation through a direct experience of unity with all of life. . . .

For a select few, an object of longing appears at once, as in Paul's revelation of blinding light on the road to Damascus, or Dante's sighting of the young Beatrice, or Ram Dass's instantaneous recognition of his Indian master, or St. Catherine's first vision of Jesus. That vision takes over the emotional life of the person like a possession. For example, Paul, formerly a Jew who fought against the teachings of Jesus, became the main advocate for a life in Christ. . . .

For some, the holy longing is felt with the sweetness of hope and the ideal of communion with others. "I long for a community of souls," a friend said, "where I'm like one lit firefly among thousands in the dark skies." For others, it is suffered with the bitterness of isolation and disillusionment. An encounter with our lower nature, our sins or shadows, may evoke a deep desire for repentance and healing. When we see our own cruelty or face our unconscious limitations for the first time, we may yearn for the light of consciousness and the forgiveness of higher forces.

> The soul is drawn by desire for god like a lover is drawn by the scent of the beloved.

Many individuals turn a deaf ear to the whispers of the soul. Myths tell us of heroes who do not heed the call. Today, too, despite their spiritual thirst, some people retrench in established patterns, too fearful to risk changing a life of comfort. Or they find substitute gratification in an addictive substance, which appears to quench their thirst for a moment. But their holy longing is simply held captive by that substance. On the other hand, stories of the mystics and saints in every tradition give us a glimpse into the lives of those who follow their longing to its source.

GOD LONGS FOR US AS WE LONG FOR GOD

IN HINDUISM, BRAHMA, the creator, manifested life to dispel the enveloping darkness. He created the waters and deposited a seed that became a golden egg, which was divided into male and female. For Hindu mystics, the purpose of life is to realize consciously the unity that was present in the beginning unconsciously....

In Jewish mysticism, the light of the absolute source, or *Ein Sof*, descended, degree by degree, into the world through many "garments," which screened its light, until the material world emerged as darkness embodied. The purpose of this downward gradation of light into creation is transformative: One day, with the coming of the Messiah, the light of the *Ein Sof* will shine in the place of greatest darkness.

But this fulfillment depends upon human action. When believers follow the commandments with the proper intention, or *kavanah*, they bring down the light from above into matter, which was previously dark.... This work of repairing the world, or *tikkun olam*, is the hidden purpose of Jewish life, and it may carry us far into the darkness of descent....

In Christianity, Paul spoke (in Philippians 3) about *epektasis*, reaching forth to the things that are before us and forgetting the things that are behind. We might interpret Paul's description of dying each day (in 1 Corinthians) as transcending the level of the past and being reborn to a new consciousness.

Early Christian saint Gregory of Nyssa wrote commentaries about *epektasis*, which he translated as straining toward god. For Gregory, this human effort, which stems from free will, takes place within the context of the soul's movement of perpetual ascent toward god, who is immovable. The soul is drawn by desire for god like a lover is drawn by the scent of the beloved, as described in the *Song of Songs*....

The sixth-century *Rule of St. Benedict* prescribed behavior that led each monk to share in the sufferings of Christ so that he deserved to share in his kingdom. But these behaviors are empty without straining forward with hope in Christ, by whose spirit we participate through grace in the nature of god. As his divine image is restored in us, we are ever more capable of giving and receiving love.

Contemporary Christian teacher Gordon Dalbey takes a more psychological approach to god as the Father. He told me, in a personal communication, that most Christians don't acknowledge their holy longing because, as children, they called out for their father and he failed them.... "Our fathers didn't come when we called, so we learned not to trust them. Some of us awaited their arrival with fear and dread. As a result, it's not safe to long for God the Father today. It's not safe to be like a little child, dependent on God. But that's exactly what we need for healing."...

For many of us, the holy longing carries the seed desire of a life story.

We can recognize these ideas in the lived realities of seekers and saints, in their narrative stories of poignant yearning for the divine beloved. Whether Christian, Jew, Hindu, Buddhist, or Sufi, whether theistic or nontheistic, they long for union with something transcendent, something beyond themselves....

What is the proper stance toward our holy longing? We might take refuge from it in our rationality, attempting to think away the discomfort of the feeling or to rationalize it as an impossible dream. Or we might embrace it with open arms but closed eyes, innocently grasping at teachers or teachings that promise transcendence, while leaving ourselves open to destructive personal or group dynamics. Or we might try to relinquish the desire to go up to spirit and seek only to go down, valuing body over spirit, darkness over light, immanence over transcendence.

Feminists might critique the holy longing for something Other as a sacrifice of individual power, becoming like an object to the divine subject and achieving fulfillment only at the price of autonomy and reason. Certainly, our religious institutions and creeds have been forces for social conservatism, appalling sexism, and even genocide. In fact, they have used our holy longing as currency, promising salvation or higher consciousness in exchange for obedience.

Postmodernists might critique it as a holdover of the modern era, when beliefs could simply be believed and egos could simply be taken to have substance. Certainly, our growing capacity to see through beliefs and our growing awareness of the mythic stature of the ego will, in the future, alter the way we describe religious experience.

But I propose that, for many of us, the holy longing carries the seed desire of a life story. If planted deeply enough in the soul, if allowed to gestate, if nurtured carefully, it may yield a rich harvest. Certainly, if one follows these seasons, this seed may lead you to the myth at the center of your life, the story that unfolds beneath your yearnings and wanderings....

To the degree that we do not take our longing into our own souls, where it truly belongs, and suffer through it as a rite of passage, we will be compelled to live it out literally to the bitter end—and to live only and always in painful longing. But if we can acknowledge our religious yearning and even befriend it, and if we can detect the hidden objects of our desire, perhaps we can follow our holy longing to a higher end.

Excerpted from *Meeting the Shadow on the Spiritual Path* by Connie Zweig, PhD published by Inner Traditions International and Bear & Company, © 2023. All rights reserved. http://www.Innertraditions.com. Reprinted with permission of publisher.

Abraham Joshua Heschel: "Moral Grandeur and Spiritual Audacity"

By Or N. Rose

January 18, 2025, (corresponding to 18 Tevet, 5785 on the Hebrew calendar) marks the fifty-second anniversary of the passing of Rabbi Abraham Joshua Heschel (1907–1972), one of the great religious figures of the twentieth century. In honor of his yahrtzeit (anniversary of death in Yiddish), I offer the following reflection on Heschel's religious activism, grounded in his theology of "Divine pathos."[1]

O N J U N E 16, 1963, the Jewish theologian and scholar Abraham Joshua Heschel sent a carefully crafted telegram to President John F. Kennedy. Rabbi Heschel did so just one day before he was to attend a gathering of religious leaders at the White House to discuss African American civil rights with the president. He intended this brief, sharply worded message to stir Kennedy and his administration to take bold action, moving beyond "solemn" declarations and modest interventions. Heschel urged the president to demand of religious leaders that they invest more of themselves in the civil rights movement, including helping to fund housing and education for Black people. He then called on Kennedy directly to launch a national initiative to address the socio-economic plight of African Americans. Echoing the prophets of ancient Israel, he closed his memo by proclaiming that "the hour calls for moral grandeur and spiritual audacity."

> To President John F. Kennedy, the White House, June 16, 1963. I look forward to privilege of being present at meeting tomorrow at 4 p.m. Likelihood exists that Negro problem will be like the weather. Everybody talks about it but nobody does anything about it. Please demand of religious leaders personal involvement not just solemn declaration. We forfeit the right to worship God as long as we continue to humiliate Negroes. Churches synagogues have failed. They must repent. Ask of religious leaders to call for national repentance and personal sacrifice. Let religious leaders donate one month's salary toward fund for Negro housing and education. I propose that you Mr. President declare state of moral emergency. A Marshall Plan for aid to Negroes is becoming a necessity. The hour calls for high moral grandeur and spiritual audacity.[2]

Before analyzing the substance of this statement, it is important to know something about the life journey of the outspoken man who wrote it.

Heschel came to the United States in 1940 under great duress, narrowly escaping the brutal Nazi onslaught in Europe. Born in Warsaw, Poland into an illustrious Hasidic family,[3] he was a doctoral student at the Friedrich Wilhelm University (today Humboldt University) and a candidate for rabbinic ordination[4] at the liberal Institute for Scientific Jewish Studies in Berlin when Hitler came to power in 1933. After being deported to Poland in 1937, Heschel received a special scholar's visa from Hebrew Union College in Cincinnati, Ohio. Broken-hearted and alone, he left Warsaw in 1938, just six weeks before Germany invaded Poland. Tragically, many of Heschel's family members—including his mother and three of his sisters—were murdered by the Nazis in the following months and years.[5] In reflecting on this agonizing turn of events, Heschel described himself as a "brand plucked from the fire in which my people were burned to death."[6]

After acculturating to life in the United States and establishing himself as a respected academic and gifted religious writer, Heschel became increasingly involved in public affairs. This included his engagement in the civil rights movement, the struggle for the religious and cultural freedom of Soviet Jewry, the Second Vatican Council, and the anti-Vietnam war movement. It was no accident that Heschel emerged as a social activist as he was working on the English adaptation of his doctoral thesis on the Hebrew prophets. Reflecting on the impact of this book project, he stated: "I've learned from the prophets that I have to be involved in the affairs of man, in the affairs of suffering man."[7] Heschel's *The Prophets*, published in 1962, was a key source of inspiration for several leaders in the civil rights movement.[8]

Our march was worship. I felt my legs were praying.

Heschel gave his first major address on civil rights in March 1963 at the National Conference on Religion and Race in Chicago. In his remarks, he compared the plight of African Americans in the United States to the ancient Israelite slaves in Egypt. In one particularly dramatic moment, he stated, "It may have been easier for the Children of Israel to cross the Red Sea than for a Negro to cross certain university campuses." He went on to challenge listeners—including many Jewish audience members—to choose between the legacies of Pharoah or Moses.[9]

It was at this conference that Heschel first met the Reverend Dr. Martin Luther King Jr. The two became close friends and colleagues and remained so until Dr. King's murder in 1968. While these men came from very different backgrounds, they shared several qualities that brought them together during a tumultuous and transformative period in American life. Both came from prominent religious families and were nurtured from a young age by their elders to lead their respective religious communities. Both were passionate believers in a God of compassion and justice, who called on humankind to serve as cocreators of a world guided by these values. Each turned to the Hebrew Bible and other sacred sources for inspiration and guidance, while also incorporating various historical-critical methods of interpretation. And both men were masterful at using their exegetical and linguistic skills to awaken people's consciousness and stir them to "love in action."[10]

Rather than turn away in rage or despair from engagement with non-Jews, Heschel became a champion of racial justice and interreligious cooperation.

In the telegram, Heschel writes with the same polemical tone as he did in his Chicago address. Here, however, he focuses on his fellow religious leaders—Jewish and Christian alike—before addressing the president directly. Heschel's assessment is both piercing and terse (as a telegram demands): "We forfeit the right to worship God as long as we continue to humiliate Negros." In fine prophetic fashion, he rails against ritual observance divorced from social responsibility. As he writes elsewhere, "Prayer is no panacea, no substitute for action."[11] While Heschel was an eloquent spokesperson for a life of disciplined religious praxis—including prayer and other traditional observances[12]—he was steadfast in his call for a *holistic* approach to spirituality and ethics. It was his hope that President Kennedy—who himself faced prejudice as the first Catholic president of the United States[13]—would be moved by this bold call for religious activism to combat bigotry and injustice.

It is also noteworthy that Heschel speaks directly about the relationship between racism and poverty, suggesting that the president develop a domestic version of the Marshall Plan to help African Americans heal from severe economic disadvantage. If the United

States could invest billions of dollars in rebuilding Europe after World War II, why could it not invest in the economic wellbeing of members of its own country who had been badly mistreated for centuries? While Heschel does not mention it explicitly, he is also urging Kennedy and his administration to support the March on Washington for Jobs and Freedom that several national groups were attempting to organize at the time. While the president was becoming more actively involved in the cause of civil rights–having just made a major television address on the subject–he was still hesitant about this mass gathering, fearing the eruption of violence and political backlash.[14]

Two years after writing this telegram to Kennedy, Heschel joined Dr. King and other civil rights leaders in the famous Selma to Montgomery March. Upon returning from that protest, he wrote the following words:

> For many of us the march from Selma to Montgomery was about protest and prayer. Legs are not lips, and marching is not kneeling, and yet our legs uttered songs. Even without words, our march was worship. I felt my legs were praying.[15]

For Heschel, marching for voting rights was a holy act, an embodied devotional response to God's ongoing call for dignity and equality. His Hasidic forebearers might have called it *avodah be'gashmiut*, "worship through corporeality."[16] Interestingly, in this brief reflection, he alternates between the singular and the plural, thus suggesting that this was a shared experience of worship–"even without words"– among people from different religious traditions.

Heschel also wrote in his diary that marching with Dr. King and the other civil rights leaders reminded him of walking with the great Hasidic masters of his youth.[17] He experienced a similar sense of nobility in his experience with his Eastern European mentors and with his North American colleagues. This comparison is itself a powerful ecumenical statement, but even more so when one considers Heschel's experiences of antisemitism–including as a child in Poland, decades before the rise of Nazism. Further, there are many negative depictions of gentiles in classical Hasidic literature, born, in part, from experiences of degradation and oppression at the hands of Christian actors.[18]

Rather than turn away in rage or despair from engagement with non-Jews, Heschel became a champion of racial justice and interreligious cooperation. He used his own experiences as a victim of bigotry and hatred to work to stamp out these destructive phenomena in his new homeland and throughout the world. As mentioned above, this included his involvement in the historic Second Vatican Council of the Catholic Church (1961–1964).[19] The following academic year (1965–1966), Heschel served as the inaugural Harry Emerson Fosdick Visiting Professor at Union Theological Seminary (Protestant). It was there that he wrote his most well-known reflection on interfaith cooperation, entitled "No Religion Is an Island."[20] In 1965–1966, Heschel also helped establish the interfaith organization Clergy and Laymen Concerned About Vietnam, recruiting Dr. King to join the cause.[21]

As a rabbi and Jewish educator immersed in various interreligious and civic initiatives, I consider Heschel to be a role model and a challenging presence in my life. Not only did he labor to revitalize Jewish spiritual life in the United States, but he also played a vital role in healing racial, religious, and political wounds in America and beyond. Further, this spiritual and ethical gadfly was motivated not only by theological conviction and historical knowledge, but by personal experience. His belief in the human capacity for compassion and justice—as beings created in the image of the Divine (see Genesis 1:27)—was severely challenged by the barbarity of the Nazis, including the murder of his family. Yet, he refused to give up on humanity. Rather than retreating and insulating himself from the aches and pains of the world, he cultivated relationships with a diverse set of colleagues and organizations and set out to help transform it.

May Rabbi Abraham Joshua Heschel's memory continue to serve as a source of inspiration and challenge to all those who seek to participate in the healing of our shared civilization.

A Holy Exile

By Michael Battle

In the wake of Archbishop Desmond Tutu's death in the Christmas season (December 26, 2021), I now vividly understand a core tenet of African spirituality much more deeply–namely, there is a fate worse than death. What do I mean? Well, of all the Christian liturgical seasons, Christmas is the most indicative of finding a home. This is well documented in the Holy Family's pursuit of a home in exile while in Egypt. Most of all, for Christian sensibilities, God makes a home in the Incarnation of Jesus. The search for a home is no less complicated two thousand years later, as many still find themselves as fugitives, "illegal aliens," and victims of political systems. A fate worse than death is found here in the inability to fully belong as a human being.

Leaders of political regimes know this all too well as they send those in opposition into exile. Instead of killing the opposition outright, those in power fear the martyr or the human witness who points to the reality of something far greater than human power. South Africa's history is chock full of these examples of the exiled, including the witness of Nelson Mandela, exiled like John of Patmos on an island surrounded by carnivorous sharks.

The far greater power witnessed in African spirituality is *anamnesis*–the power of remembering the ancestors. Christians practice this power in the Eucharist, which constantly reminds us that we are more than the sum of individuals. There is a life form that comes alive by simply belonging to each other. Similar to remembering the communion of saints, the insight of remembrance is in how such an act of re-membering keeps persons and communities alive. Acts of re-membrance are not superficial or somehow childish psychological coping mechanisms. Rather, they are vital for human flourishing. In contrast, the goal of evil is to dis-member the other by normalizing the idea that someone should never exist. Evil's purpose is to dehumanize another to the point of making it easy and necessary to turn a person into an object of destruction. If the person is not destroyed, then the second-best outcome for evil is to objectify the other as a slave for personal gain. This also is a fate worse than death.

God would not exist unless there is someone to love. In such love, we are all invited out of exile and into the holy life.

Tutu's life fiercely resisted these evil outcomes. Tutu's contemplative life, comingled with an *ubuntu* politic, was a practice of exorcism—namely, exposing evil for what it is. Evil loses its power when fully seen. Tutu's life of praying the daily office and participating in a daily Eucharist helped him to contemplate the divine miracle of how all of us (enemies included) could practice being persons together (*ubuntu*, an African definition of humanity through the axiom, *I am because you are*). No one need be exiled.

Since Tutu's passing, I am pleased to see that he is being remembered around the world in conversations about *ubuntu*, restorative justice, truth and reconciliation, interreligious dialogue, forgiveness, and a spirituality of justice. My aim in this reflection, however, is to remember Tutu's holy life because such remembrance is sadly rare.

Also, unfortunately for some still exiled in this world, a holy life is a ludicrous proposition. Church leadership is seen in secular society today as a swinging pendulum between a Monty Python sketch and a Jordan Peele horror movie. In short, the church's ability to replicate a life form beyond its individual parts is rarely seen. As a result, it is rare to admit that holy people exist, much less to celebrate them. Unfortunately, holy people are in exile or continue to run toward Egypt.

Holy people being in exile is a most tragic circumstance because, if we are not careful, they can easily be forgotten, which is a fate worse than death. My aim in restoring the exiled is the same as Paul the Apostle in his conversation with Timothy—namely, when pursuing what a spiritual leader looks like, do not look for a conceited person who naturally embraces absolute power. Rather, look for someone whose frame of reference is outside that person's affinity group. Finding honor outside one's own tribe is, strangely enough, favorable and honorable, as seen in St. Paul's plea for congeniality between Jew and Gentile. We can learn from holy people like Paul, who did not see himself as holy, but as one in exile. Paul's goal was to break the paradigm of the exiled and encourage us to live a holy life that actually may attract "outsiders" to God (1 Timothy 3:6–7). In the same way, we break the paradigm of the exiled by celebrating Tutu's life. Yet, to celebrate such a life comes with many challenges, even within the Christian family itself. For example, many want to forget Tutu's life witness by categorizing him only as a politician. This sparked the so-called Christian pastor Jerry Falwell (1933–2007) to say, "Tutu is phony."[1]

As St. Paul directed Timothy, not only should a holy person find honor outside of that person's natural communities, but that person should also be honored in that person's own hometown as well. If we are not careful, the church can easily become the power that exiles the most people. Christians can easily become the most unforgiving in this respect, as so many people in the world are neither recognized nor celebrated "in the name of God."

The good news, however, is that Tutu elicited an abundance of respect for the church. In 1976, when Tutu served as General Secretary of the South African Council of Churches, an interesting event occurred. He had to face a tribunal in Pretoria that sought to discredit Tutu's spiritual authority. This court turned over every stone in search of scandal and hypocrisy in Tutu's life. The inquisitor's questions were grueling as Tutu sat alone in a chair at a little table, facing the tribunal for twenty hours. At one of the hearings, there was a commotion during which a strange gathering of people inserted themselves into the courtroom's public gallery. They were representatives of the Archbishop of Canterbury, the Pope in Rome, the World Council of Churches, the National Council of Churches in the United States, the World Methodist Conference, the World Lutheran Federation, and the World Alliance of Reformed Churches. Like the biblical Magi carrying gifts, they traveled from great distances to South Africa to be present as witnesses that Tutu was indeed true and holy and not laughable and evil. Suddenly, the tribunal kangaroo court knew it was taking on the church around the world.

In God, no one is exiled.

In my recent book on Tutu, I based Tutu's longevity and productivity on his spirituality, going so far as to state that Tutu is a saint.[2] This is controversial, because Tutu was hit hard by both sides in the monumental conflicts he faced: conservative and liberal, black and white, religious and political, North and South, and rich and poor. What held him together in these maelstroms was God, and what made Tutu holy was God. Any controversy around who deserves to be a saint is resolved by the theological fact that no one *deserves* to be a saint, but is only *made* into a saint.

In my research on Tutu's theology, I constantly read how Tutu perceived God as pulsating love from all eternity. For Tutu, God is a fellowship, a community, not an individual or modality. God is unified because love binds the three persons of God together. So, God created us the same way—out of love, not out of necessity. Herein is one of Tutu's greatest contributions to how a holy life moves out of exile—namely, no one can be human alone. Tutu witnessed to how God is necessary being, whereas we are contingent human beings who depend utterly on God's love. But here's the thing: God too is necessarily dependent on love. As I state in my forthcoming book, *Ubuntu: An Atonement Theology*, God would not exist unless there is someone to love. In such love, we are all invited out of exile and into the holy life. Tutu witnessed to the theological fact that because of love, we are all created to be saints.

Tutu believed that we are privileged to be God's eucharistic (thankful) persons who hold everything in trust for God and who are forever saying thank you for God's generosity. We return to God what God entrusted to us temporarily–time, money, talent, and life. We live into a holy life by seeking to reflect God's own lavish and magnificent generosity, which in turn invites us into eternal life.

I heard Tutu preach often when I served as his chaplain. One of his common refrains was that *each of us* represents God, not just the clever, the strong, the rich, the beautiful, the tall, or the impressive ones. Every Tom, Dick, and Harry, Mary and Jane of us. Tutu would go on to explain how monumental this was in terms of a paradigm shift–namely that in God, no one is exiled. Now, the old black lady that cleans houses and takes care of white children, whose employers do not even use her real name "because it is too difficult" and simply call her a generic name like Mary or Jane–when she walks down the street, and people ask, "Who's that?" she will now think with her head in her heart, "I am God's representative." This is what I mean by Tutu's holy life: He facilitated the perspective in others, even among those despised on this planet, that they are holy people. This was Tutu's genius–that everyone, religious and nonreligious, friend and enemy, are all created in the image of God.

It also must be said of Tutu's holy life that he said his prayers. He didn't pray ostentatiously, which Jesus warned against, but through his daily disciplines and rule of life. Tutu prayed the way my Apple watch makes me stop and breathe deeply several times a day. In addition to the Anglican daily office, Tutu recognized the wisdom of the Eastern world that prayer is tied to how we breathe. We all have the spirit of life breathed into us, and life is thus a gift from God. For Tutu, we become God's breath in the world in order to transfigure creation to look like the Creator. I can still hear Tutu say, in his pastoral visits to churches, that you and I are placed in this world of hatred, violence, anger, injustice, and oppression to help God transform it, transfigure it, and change it so that there will be compassion, laughter, joy, peace, reconciliation, fellowship, friendship, togetherness, and family, and so that black and white people would want to be together as members of one family: God's family, the human family. We are here to bring others out of exile.

You and I are placed in this world of hatred, violence, anger, injustice, and oppression to help God transform it, transfigure it, and change it.

Tutu's Christian imagination could only come from the process of becoming holy. One must have eyes to see and understand this, even if it appears naïve and delusional. I think Tutu's eyes were opened as he continued the crucial discipline in his life of saying his prayers every day. When he said his prayers, he recognized the fullness of life in which there was no narcissism or sibling rivalry. When Tutu prayed, he believed that God does not look at us as we are in our own eyes, but as we are loved by God, who created our eyes in the first place.

My aim and appeal to Tutu's holy life must also adhere to the power of community that continually awakens the good news that there will be a new heaven and a new earth in which no one gets lost and no one is exiled. In our proclivity toward relativism, community remains true only in our practice of properly relating one precious identity to another. Our identities are precious because we are made in the image of God's identity.

It seems to me that there indeed must be intentional efforts to honor Tutu's life by remembering *ubuntu*. Not only is this theologically sound as it pertains to God, but it is also sound politically, economically, medically, and in so many other ways. Tutu's holy life calls us all to community so that we may all have a future. The strength of Tutu's life is in the expansive truths of God within the gathering of people. When religion is used as centrifugal force to move people away from each other, we have lost Tutu's genius. Tutu's theology of community provides a synchronic function in so many aspects of how to be healthy human beings.

Tutu did not see himself as a saint. No real saint ever does. Instead, he lived in the constant conflicts of this rough-and-tumble world in such a way that we now, in hindsight, see his pearls of great price. The tensions and agitations in Tutu's life produced these pearls, and the good news for us is that he inspires such pearls in our own lives. This seems to be an important function in a holy life: to remind the living that we too can be holy.

Tutu's life is attractive for any spiritual or moral compass because his life is one of those rare examples in religion in which someone is actually *for you*, not against. Such an attractive person has to train for this because many of the desires in this world only operate on the basis of being for self or a self's version of God. The reason I find Tutu so appealing is that he seemed to realize the risk of his enterprise of being for you as well as what is at stake if no one is for you. Ultimately, Tutu's holiness comes from his perspective of God, who is *for all* of us to move out of exile.

Never Alone

By Randy S. Woodley

WE ARE NEVER alone. I say this not as some comforting platitude. Rather, I am stating a fact of human existence. After nearly three thousand years of influence from Platonic dualism, we may feel the pressure to think we are alone. That's because this harmful philosophy, now a Western lifeway, has created a sense of superiority over all our nonhuman relatives. The word for this is anthropocentrism, meaning humans view themselves as distinct from and better than the rest of creation, but we are not.

Here's how Platonic dualism worked on us to achieve a false state of the possibility of being alone. Platonic dualism taught us that the mind is superior to the body and other physicalities, such as nature. This teaching, that eventually became our Western reality, led us on a path of ranking various aspects of our existence in hierarchies. If our reality was mind over matter, thinking above doing, the ethereal over the material, then everything else in life could be ranked in hierarchies. This new reality always ranked human beings over the rest of creation.

It justified a mentality of extraction from creation as opposed to living with creation in a symbiotic relationship.

Indigenous people have no hierarchy of humanity over the rest of creation.

A worldview of Platonic dualism was easily molded to wield power in this new reality. Men could have a "natural" sway over women and refer to them as the "weaker vessel." Light-skinned Europeans could feel "naturally" superior to darker, more exotic human beings, classifying them as savages, barbarians, and heathens. This is the fount from which scientific racism grew and bestowed upon humanity West African chattel slavery, genocide of Native Americans, the Third Reich, Apartheid, and Jim Crow.

Platonic dualism deeply affected the Western church, creating an overemphasis on doctrine and a lack of accountability to ethics and actions. Overall, Western Christian theologies became disembodied. It became more important in life to give assent to correct doctrine (orthodoxy) than to reflect the character of Jesus in one's everyday life (orthopraxis). Western Christians became so obsessed with orthodoxy that they split the body of Christ into manifold pieces, creating new and more precise doctrinal statements, denominations, and even wars against those with opposing views where they killed one another, supposedly to protect the truth of Christ.

I blame Platonic dualism for splitting reality for the Western worldview. The reason for my accusation comes with a comparison, because Indigenous people around the world, who were not affected as severely by the Western worldview, do not have this split in reality. By and large, Indigenous people understand the physical, material world to be equal to and essentially part of our whole reality. Indigenous people have no hierarchy of humanity over the rest of creation. We understand that we all—humans and the rest of the whole community of creation—have equal purpose. We do not view women to be somehow lower than men. In fact, in most Indigenous societies, women play key roles, as do men. Indigenous people understand people who are different as having different views and giftings, all of which are valuable.

I make the comparison, not to say Indigenous people have a utopian existence or are somehow better than other societies, but merely to point out that an Indigenous worldview has not been affected by Platonic dualism to the extent that the Western worldview has. In this regard, I will say an Indigenous worldview has a better grip on the whole of reality than the Western worldview, which leads me back to my opening statement: We are never alone.

In many societies, especially Indigenous societies, our oldest stories speak of animals talking among themselves. Sometimes they even talk with humans and allow humans to get to know them. These stories speak of a relationship built on equity, with each species having a role to play. All beings are vital for the cooperation of harmony in the community of creation. One such story is found in the book of Genesis in the Hebrew Bible.

The Creator tells the first human to name the animals. Adam, the namer, is himself named from his most obvious characteristic, Red Earth, as he is made from the dirt. In turn, Red Earth Man must travel through the garden of creation and observe the rest of creation. The command is to get to know the community of creation and name them according to their characteristics. Even today, Indigenous peoples have stories that emphasize these characteristics, like how the possum lost its beautiful tail or how the raccoon got a black mask. Only by getting to know the rest of the community of creation can we give them proper names, befitting their importance to the rest of the community of creation.

In Creator's purview, everyone has a purpose and is worth knowing. This is the worldview the West has lost. We are not above or below the rest of the community of creation. We are simply a part of it. But our role, that of caretakers, of co-sustainers, is vital. It is our role to keep the rest of the community of creation in harmony and balance. Among my tribe, we have a story that speaks to this directly. It goes like this:

> In the old days, all the animals, birds, fish, and plants could talk, and everyone lived together in peace and friendship under the delight of the Creator. But after a while, the humans began to spread over the whole earth. The animals, birds, fish, and plants found themselves beginning to be cramped for room. This was

bad enough, but then humans began to needlessly slaughter the animals (including birds, insects, reptiles, etc.), becoming wasteful.

The humans no longer thanked the Creator-Great Mystery for supplying food, nor did they thank the animals for feeding human families through the giving of their lives. Every traditional Cherokee knows that it is considered polite to thank the Creator and thank the animal when it furnishes its own life so people may eat and sustain their lives for another day.

So, to protect themselves from the evil that had come upon them from the once-grateful Cherokee, the animals resolved to hold a council to discuss their common survival.

The council was first led by the bears. The Great White Bear asked, "How do the people kill us?" "With bows and arrows," someone replied. "Then we must make bows and arrows," declared the leader. But soon, the bears found they could not shoot straight with their large claws getting in the way, and they needed their claws to dig for grubs and such. Finally, the rest of the animals lost confidence in the bears' leadership, and they elected the inchworm to convene the gathering. The inchworm listened carefully to what the rest of the animals had to say.

After much debate, the animals decided to bring diseases upon the Cherokee people. The animals were creative, thinking of smallpox, chicken pox, swine flu, bird flu, and many other diseases. The Cherokee people began getting sick and dying from these diseases. First it was the children and old people who began to die. Then the men and even the strong women died. The Cherokee's future looked very bleak.

After many Cherokees had died, they pleaded with the animals, "Please, we will become grateful and kill only that which we will eat." But the animals would not take back the diseases they had created to kill the Cherokee.

At the same time, the plants were watching all these things. They watched as the Cherokee children and old people got sick. Once the strong warriors and even the women were dying, the plants decided to hold a council. In the council, they agreed to provide medicine for the Cherokee. Each night, as the Cherokees would sleep, the plants would come to them in their dreams and show them how to use the plants to heal the diseases that the animals had brought upon them.

The Cherokees recovered, and there was a great council held between the human people, the animal people, and the plant people. The human people agreed always to kill only what they absolutely needed. They also agreed to put down tobacco and say a prayer of thanks to any animal that they killed and to any plant that would be harvested for food, housing, or medicine.

The Creator was happy with the Cherokees once again because harmony was restored among all that Creator-Great Mystery had created.

Each one of us may draw different conclusions from this story, but hopefully, we all see the interdependence being taught between humans and the rest of the community of creation. I think this is also present in the Genesis story, when Adam is told to name the animals. In this story, Creator-Great Mystery is urging the humans to understand their relationship with the rest of creation and to realize that they are not alone, but exist within a great community of creation, each having a particular role to play in the grand scheme of things.

All beings are vital for the cooperation of harmony in the community of creation.

My wife and I are farmers, among other roles we play, but farming has been a key to our understanding of this principle of living in the whole community of creation. The seeds we plant and keep are sometimes referred to as our babies, as are the young plants. We talk of the new starts in the greenhouse as "the babies." One of us will ask the other, "Honey, have you checked on the babies today?" As the plants grow and mature, we water them and be sure they are getting enough sun or are protected from the cold. We understand our role as co-sustaining the plants.

While we are farming, we are visited by various birds, including songbirds, woodpeckers, hawks, and eagles, all of whom fly overhead or land near us and give us a song while we are tending the plant people. Our hands are digging deep in the soil, breaching layers of earth–first warm, then cool–and we are reminded that the soil itself is alive. Each handful of dirt contains millions of live bacteria and miles of fungi strands, all hidden from the naked eye, and yet, they are there. This is when we realize we are simply farm helpers. Those billions of bacteria, protozoa, anthropoids, and mycelium in the soil are doing the real work of bringing health to the soil. Part of our role is to be sure the soil is fed and balanced properly so they can do their job. We all work together. We are never alone.

With such a wonderful and diverse community of creation available to every human being, we should ask ourselves, when we are lonely, how much time we have spent getting to know our nonhuman neighbors. How are they doing? Are they struggling? In what ways might we make life better for them? Perhaps we can even go deeper than their physical needs. How are they experiencing life, emotionally and spiritually?

Wait! Do animals have a spiritual life? We know they have emotions. Anyone who has ever had a pet dog or cat can sense in it deep emotions of happiness, sadness, anger, shame, and a whole plethora of emotions. But spirituality?

In one of the most depressing, despairing, and loneliest times of my life, a deer spoke to me. I was in the woods in Wisconsin, expressing my angst to Creator, and a baby fawn walked into the same clearing in which I was sitting. It lay down about thirty feet from me and just looked at me with its big brown eyes. I kept watching it, wondering why it was not afraid. Finally, a deep thought that was more like a voice–not my voice, but still, from my heart–sounded in my spirit. The deer spoke to me without moving its mouth or head, and I heard it clearly. It was Creator, speaking through the deer. I won't say here what it said, but that simple phrase changed my life, and I have never been the same since. That spotted fawn changed the direction of my life's path forever.

If a baby deer can be used by Creator to make such a distinct change in my life, I would never deny that it has a spirituality. An animal's spirituality may be different than mine, but I recognize it just the same. As I look around the community of creation, I notice rocks, trees, the sun, and the wind, all of whom have the potential to speak to me because they are inhabited by Spirit–and Spirit is everywhere.

We are never alone.

RECOMMENDED READING

Borders and Belonging: The Book of Ruth:
A Story for Our Times

Pádraig Ó Tuama and Glenn Jordan
Canterbury Press, 2021

A Book Review by Lee Staman

Pádraig Ó Tuama, a poet and theologian, partnered with Glenn Jordan, a program manager for public theology, to write a book in the midst of Brexit that would help people make sense of the contemporary issues of migration, borders, identity, and the other. They took as their starting point the book of Ruth, an often-overlooked book that appears in the Hebrew Bible and the Christian Old Testament. Writing alternating chapters, Ó Tuama and Jordan (who passed away suddenly in 2020, before the book was published), each lend their expertise to interpret the story of Ruth for our times, engaging directly with modern-day questions of migration, refugee crises, and the social dynamics of belonging.

In just four short chapters, the Book of Ruth tells the story of a Moabite woman, living during the time of the Judges of ancient Israel, who must come to terms with the death of her Israelite husband. She chooses to go to Judah with her mother-in-law, Naomi, instead of returning to her homeland of Moab. The story of Ruth is one of great loss, migration, survival, and inclusion. As Jordan puts it, "Not only is she an ethnic stranger, she is also a woman in a man's world, a foreigner in a country that doesn't like her sort, childless in a society that required sons, a widow in a family-based culture and poor in a community that lacked a comprehensive safety net. She is therefore uniquely vulnerable."[1]

Ruth's decision to journey with Naomi to Bethlehem in Judah–despite being a foreigner–marks the beginning of a story about loyalty, kinship, and integration. Ruth's story, in which she is both a stranger and an essential part of the Israelite community, offers a powerful metaphor for understanding belonging and the possibilities of social transformation. By focusing on Ruth's status as a foreigner, a widow, and a marginalized woman, the authors make a direct connection between the biblical narrative and the lived experiences of many people in today's world–particularly those displaced by war, poverty, or systemic injustice. They also make a point regarding the place of Ruth within the Jewish liturgy. It is told alongside the massive epic that is the book of Exodus with the reasoning that, "Maybe this is why we are invited to read it [Exodus] alongside the human-scale story of Ruth. It reminds us to keep our eyes and ears alert for the small dramas that constitute the lives of most and to avoid being distracted by the hoopla of the dancing mountain."[2]

The central message of the book is that the story of Ruth can offer important insights into how communities and individuals can respond to the "stranger" or "other" in their midst, especially in an era marked by anti-immigrant sentiment and rising nationalism. The authors explore Ruth's movement across borders–not only in a literal geographical sense but also in a social and cultural one. Ruth is not just crossing physical borders. She is moving between different understandings of identity, religion, and belonging. In a similar way, many modern migrants are forced to navigate shifting boundaries of language, culture, and legal status. As Jordan writes, "The book of Ruth reminds us to look to the margins and to ask about who is being affected by these global eruptions."[3] He goes on to say that we must "train the ears of the participants for the thin voices of those who struggle to find their footing in troubled times."[4]

Another important aspect of the Book of Ruth that the authors focus on is the intersection of gender and belonging. Ruth is not only a foreigner. She is also a woman in a patriarchal society. The story of Ruth, Naomi, and Boaz demonstrates how women navigate spaces of power, survival, and opportunity. Ruth's agency–her decisions to move, to work, and to seek out justice–is integral to the unfolding of the story. In many ways, Ruth becomes a model of empowerment for marginalized groups, particularly women, who find ways to survive and even thrive in environments that are not necessarily welcoming or just. Ó Tuama and Jordan point out, "In a time of judging judges, someone has chosen to write a story where a woman's courage is the thing that returns a people to themselves."[5]

In *Borders and Belonging*, Ó Tuama and Jordan offer a powerful reflection on the ancient biblical narrative, showing its relevance to contemporary struggles around migration, identity, and inclusion. By reading Ruth through these lenses, the authors invite readers to reconsider how we, as individuals and communities, respond to those who are different, displaced, or excluded. The story of Ruth, they suggest, is not just about one woman's journey into a new land, but about the larger social processes of welcome, transformation, and justice. Ultimately, the book challenges readers to think critically about the borders that divide us—whether physical, cultural, or ideological—and to actively work toward building more inclusive, compassionate communities. Ó Tuama and Jordan stress, "In both a personal and political sense, a person needs to be seen. Ruth seeks to be seen. She does not come with threat to the people in this new borderland. She comes with love, but also honesty: she is honest about the truth that she sees herself as belonging, even if others do not."[6]

CONTRIBUTORS

Brian D. McLaren is Dean of CAC Faculty and a former evangelical pastor. Championing a more loving, inclusive, and contemplative Christianity, he teaches ways to reconnect with Jesus' message–unconditional love. He is author of *Faith After Doubt* and *The Great Spiritual Migration* and host of CAC's podcast *Learning How to See*.

Dr. Carmen Acevedo Butcher is an award-winning translator and teacher, poet, contemplative workshop leader, and CAC Affiliate Faculty member. She holds a doctorate in Medieval Studies from the University of Georgia and teaches at the University of California, Berkeley. She has translated Brother Lawrence's *Practice of the Presence*, *Cloud of Unknowing*, Hildegard of Bingen, and others. Visit www.carmenbutcher.com.

Mirabai Starr is an award-winning author of creative nonfiction and contemporary translations of sacred literature. She teaches and speaks internationally on contemplative practice and inter-spiritual dialogue. A certified bereavement counselor, Mirabai helps mourners harness the transformational power of loss. She lives with her extended family in the mountains of northern New Mexico.

Paul Swanson is Manager of Faculty Relations and Development at CAC and a vowed member of the Community of the Incarnation. Paul and his wife Laura have two feral, but beloved, children who are keenly aware of their impious monastic impulses. Learn more about Paul's work kindling the examined life for contemplatives at www.contemplify.com.

Barbara C. Otero-López is Director of Programs at CAC. She is a lifelong learner whose passion for nurturing learning for others inspired her doctoral study of Learning Science at the University of New Mexico and has allowed her to work as a program manager, instructional designer, curriculum developer, and teacher.

Pamela Ayo Yetunde is a pastoral counselor in private practice, and a profoundly grateful Dr. Barbara Holmes protégé. She is the author of the forthcoming *Dearly Beloved: Prince, Spirituality, and This Thing Called Life*. Ayo is also the author of *Casting Indra's Net: Fostering Spiritual Kinship and Community*.

Rosemerry Wahtola Trommer is a poet, teacher, speaker, writing facilitator, and poet laureate of Evermore. Her poems have appeared on *A Prairie Home Companion*, *PBS News Hour*, *O Magazine*, *American Life in Poetry*, *Washington Post's Book Club*, and Carnegie Hall stage. Her newest book is *The Unfolding*. One-word mantra: Adjust.

Belden Lane is Professor Emeritus of Theological Studies, American Religion, and History of Spirituality at Saint Louis University. He is the author of *Backpacking with the Saints: Wilderness Hiking as Spiritual Practice*, *The Solace of Fierce Landscapes: Exploring Desert and Mountain Spirituality*, and *Ravished by Beauty: The Surprising Legacy of Reformed Spirituality*.

Connie Zweig, PhD, is author of the award-winning book *The Inner Work of Age: Shifting from Role to Soul*, *Meeting the Shadow on the Spiritual Path: The Dance of Darkness and Light in Our Search for Awakening*, and *A Moth to the Flame: The Story of Sufi Poet Rumi*.

Rabbi Or N. Rose is founding Director of the Betty Ann Greenbaum Miller Center for Interreligious Learning & Leadership of Hebrew College, senior consultant to Interfaith America, and a CAC Affiliate Faculty member. He is publisher of *The Journal of Interreligious Studies* and co-editor of *My Neighbor's Faith* and *With the Best of Intentions*.

The Very Rev. Michael Battle is Extraordinary Professor at the Desmond Tutu Centre for Religion and Social Justice, the University of the Western Cape, South Africa; Theologian in Community at Trinity Church, Boston; and former Herbert Thompson Professor of Church and Society and Director of the Desmond Tutu Center at General Theological Seminary.

Randy S. Woodley, A CAC Affiliate Faculty Member, is the cofounder, with his wife, Edith, of Eloheh Indigenous Center for Earth Justice and Eloheh Farm & Seeds in Yamhill, Oregon. He is a Cherokee descendent recognized by the United Keetoowah Band and is Distinguished

Professor of Faith and Culture Emeritus at Portland Seminary. See eloheh.org.

Lee Staman, MLIS, is the library director at the CAC, doing research, acquisitions, cataloguing, and reference work for staff, faculty, students, alumni, and the public. He has a background in theology and philosophy and lives in Seattle, Washington with his family.

NOTES

Islands of Sanity

1. Hannah Arendt, *The Origins of Totalitarianism* (Harcourt Brace Jovanovich, 1973), 50.
2. Michael Lewis, "Has Anyone Seen the President?" *Bloomberg*, February 9, 2018, https://www.bloomberg.com/view/articles/2018-02-09/has-anyone-seen-the-president.
3. See Brian McLaren, *Why Don't They Get It? Overcoming Bias in Others (and Yourself)* and *The Second Pandemic: Authoritarianism and Your Future*, available at https://brianmclaren.net/store, and *Learning How to See* podcast, https://cac.org/podcast/learning-how-to-see/.
4. Sarah Kendzior, "We're Heading into Dark Times. This Is How to Be Your Own Light in the Age of Trump," *The Correspondent*, November 18, 2016, https://thecorrespondent.com/5696/were-heading-into-dark-times-this-is-how-to-be-your-own-light-in-the-age-of-trump/1611114266432-e23ea1a6.
5. Kendzior, "We're Heading into Dark Times."
6. Kendzior, "We're Heading into Dark Times."

A Hospitable Soul and a Well-Said Word in a Hostile Time

1. Thomas Merton, *Bread in the Wilderness* (Burns & Oates, 1954), 35.
2. Carmen Acevedo Butcher, *Man of Blessing: A Life of Saint Benedict* (Paraclete, 2012). This book on Benedict tells his life through stories and introduces readers also to his Monte Cassino monastery, twin sister Scholastica, meeting with the Goth King Totila, and more. The book includes a map, timelines, chapter-by-chapter summary of the *Rule*, and outline of a monk's day.

3 Reflecting on Umbria's beauty as shared by Benedict and Francis, seven centuries apart, a quote comes to mind from G. K. Chesterton: "What Benedict stored, Francis scattered," quoted in Richard Rohr, *Eager to Love* (Franciscan Media, 2014), 54. Read "Brother Sun, Sister Moon," also known as "Canticle of the Creatures," at https://bit.ly/FrancisSong.

4 From Horace's *Odes*, quoted in Acevedo Butcher, *Man of Blessing*, 45.

5 Ann Gibbons, "Why 536 Was 'the Worst Year to Be Alive,'" *Science*, November 15, 2018, https://www.science.org/content/article/why-536-was-worst-year-be-alive.

6 Quoted in Acevedo Butcher, *Man of Blessing*, 48.

7 For more on Gregory's complex understanding of miracles, see Acevedo Butcher, *Man of Blessing*, 21-25, 26-30, and 48-52. Gregory exercises restraint toward the miracles reported to him by monks who had known Benedict. He uses these to shed light on Benedict's pastoral approach.

8 "James Finley, "The Prophetic Path," *Richard Rohr's Daily Meditations*, September 26, 2023, (Center for Action and Contemplation, 2023), *YouTube*, 6:05.

9 Conversation with the Rev. Dr. Michael Petrow, Director of Formation, Faculty, and Foundations, Center for Action and Contemplation, February 29, 2024.

10 Richard Rohr, *A Lever and a Place to Stand* (Paulist Press, 2011), 1-4.

11 This quotation is translated (sans ellipses) by Carmen Acevedo Butcher from a letter to Marcellinus.

12 Thomas Merton, *Bread in the Wilderness* (Burns & Oates, 1954), 125.

13 Acevedo Butcher, *Man of Blessing*, 147.

14 Malcolm Gladwell, *Blink: The Power of Thinking Without Thinking* (Little Brown, 2005), 33–34.

15 For more on Benedict's *Rule*, see chapter 15 of Acevedo Butcher, *Man of Blessing*, "Writing Down a Little Rule."

Luminous Darkness

1 Mirabai Starr, trans., *Dark Night of the Soul: Saint John of the Cross* (Riverhead, 2002), 117.

2 Starr, *Dark Night*, 117.

The Monastic Impulse Leads to Unintentional Menageries in Love

1. Douglas E. Christie, *The Insurmountable Darkness of Love* (Oxford University Press, 2022), 55.
2. Brother John, "*Monos–A Greek Word Made Flesh*," *Weston Priory*, September 2019, https://www.westonpriory.org/bulletins/fw2019-9.pdf.
3. While honoring the legacy and desire for traditional monastic ways of life to flourish now and in future renewals.
4. The third monastic vow, *conversatio morum*, is often translated as "conversion of life," although its meaning is debated with fervor. It points to fidelity with a single-hearted quest for God with an openness to ongoing conversion.
5. Laura Swan, *The Wisdom of the Beguines: The Forgotten Story of a Medieval Women's Movement* (Blubridge, 2014), 12.
6. Christie, *The Insurmountable Darkness of Love*, 202.
7. The male counterparts were called *Beghards*, but they did not capture my imagination and the *joie de vivre* as the Beguines did.
8. Swan, *The Wisdom of the Beguines*, 69.
9. Swan, *The Wisdom of the Beguines*, 71–80.
10. Swan, *The Wisdom of the Beguines*, 94.
11. Swan, *The Wisdom of the Beguines*, 92.
12. Swan, *The Wisdom of the Beguines*, 151.
13. Swan, *The Wisdom of the Beguines*, 170–173.
14. Raimundo Panikkar, *Blessed Simplicity: The Monk as Universal Archetype* (Seabury, 1982), 6.15
15. See the CAC's Eight Core Principles at https://cac.org/about/the-eight-core-principles/.
16. Hindsight tells me I should have gotten the internship before quitting my job.
17. Swan, *The Wisdom of the Beguines*, 98.
18. Check out the Community of the Incarnation at spiritualimagination.org/the-community.
19. Joan Chittister, *The Monastic Heart: 50 Simple Practices for a Contemplative and Fulfilling Life* (Convergent, 2021), 82–83. (Do read the entirety of Chapter 16, "Community" in *The Monastic Heart*. She will spin your head right on the significance of community on the spiritual path.)

20 David James Duncan, *Sun House* (Hachette, 2023), 693–694.
21 Duncan, *Sun House*, 367.
22 Duncan, *Sun House*, 233.
23 Christie, *The Insurmountable Darkness of Love*, 205.
24 Duncan, *Sun House*, 495.
25 Christie, *The Insurmountable Darkness of Love*, 33.

Listen

1 Barbara Holmes, "Living in a Crowded Cosmos," *Essentials of Engaged Contemplation*, Trimester 3, Center for Action and Contemplation Living School.
2 Robert William Piatt, Jr. and Moises Gonzales, *Slavery in the Southwest: Genízaro Identity, Dignity and the Law* (Carolina Academic Press, 2019), 6.
3 Andrés Reséndez, *The Other Slavery: The Uncovered Story of Indian Enslavement in America* (HarperCollins, 2017), 55.
4 Barbara Holmes, "Living in a Crowded Cosmos," *Essentials of Engaged Contemplation*, Trimester 3, Center for Action and Contemplation Living School.

Letter to the Parts of Me I Have Tried to Exile

1 Rosemerry Wahtola Trommer, "Letter to the Parts of Me I Have Tried to Exile," © 2024, previously unpublished.

The Countercultural Spirituality of the Desert Christians

1 *Agrupnia*, meaning "wakefulness" (literally, "not asleep") is contrasted here with *apatheia* or "detachment" (literally "without passion"). These two terms are chosen for contrast because of the preference of the alpha privative or negative form in the history of the apophatic tradition. Two other words in Greek are used to describe *agrupnia* or attentiveness. *Prosochi* refers to "vigilance" or "attention"; *nipsis* carries a sense of "watchfulness" or "sobriety." See G. E. H. Palmer, Philip Sherrard, and Kallistos Ware, eds., *The Philokalia* (Faber & Faber, 1979), 1:366.
2 *Apatheia* is defined here as "indifference," not after the ancient Stoic pattern of impassiveness but after the early Christian use of the word as referring to one's struggle with temptation in the spiritual life. Active indifference became a way of focusing one's attention on that which was most worthy of love. See G. Bardy, "Apatheia," in Marcel

Viller, ed., *Dictionnaire de Spiritualité, Ascétique et Mystique: Doctrine et Histoire* (Beauchesne, 1937–1995), 1:744.

3 T. S. Eliot, *Complete Poems and Plays* (Harcourt, Brace & World, 1971), 61.

4 John Climacus, *The Ladder of Divine Ascent*, trans. Colm Luibheid and Norman Russell (Paulist, 1982), Steps 20, 29; 196–198, 282–285.

5 Stanley Hauerwas and William Willimon, *Resident Aliens* (Abingdon, 1992), 93.

6 The sayings of the fathers are filled with stories of older monks who readily sacrificed their notoriety in the spiritual life for the sake of younger brothers. In one case, a revered master even went with a younger monk to a brothel, pretending to be tempted to sin along with him in order to talk the prostitute into dissuading him from breaking his vows. *Apophthegmata Patrum*, The Sayings of the Fathers, as quoted in Columba Stewart, ed., *The World of the Desert Fathers* (SLG Press, 1986), 3–4.

7 *Apophthegmata Patrum*, The Sayings of the Fathers, in F. Nau, *Revue de L'Orient Chrétien* (1912), 206. See Benedicta Ward, *Wisdom of the Desert Fathers* (SLG Press, 1975), 50.

8 It was in this vein that Thomas Merton spoke of the contemplative as "anarchist" or outlaw, cutting against the grain of a dominant culture. *Wisdom of the Desert* (New Directions, 1970), 4–5.

9 Climacus, *The Ladder of Divine Ascent*, Step 30; 287.

10 Climacus, *The Ladder of Divine Ascent*, Step 30; 286– 287.

The Holy Longing

1 C.G. Jung, *The Psychology of Kundalini Yoga: Notes on the Seminar Given in 1932* (Princeton University Press: 2012), 34.

2 As quoted in Herbert Weiner, *9 ½ Mystics: The Kabbala Today* (Simon & Schuster, 1997), 4.

Abraham Joshua Heschel: "Moral Grandeur and Spiritual Audacity"

1 This essay is based on several earlier pieces I wrote on Heschel, including "Spirituality & Social Justice: Abraham Joshua Heschel's Telegram to JFK" in Or N. Rose, Homayra Ziad, and Soren M. Hessler, eds., *Words to Live By: Sacred Sources for Interreligious Engagement* (Orbis, 2018), 109–113.

2 This telegram has been published several times, including in Susannah Heschel, ed., *Abraham Joshua Heschel: Essential Writings* (Orbis,

2011), 64–65.

3 To learn about this popular Jewish mystical revival movement, see David Biale et al., *Hasidism: A New History* (Yale University Press, 2017).

4 He received traditional *s'mikhah* (rabbinic ordination, "laying of hands," see Numbers 27:18–23) from his Hasidic teachers as a teenager.

5 See Susannah Heschel's introduction to *Abraham Joshua Heschel: Essential Writings*, as well as Edward K. Kaplan, *Abraham Joshua Heschel: Mind, Heart, Soul* (Jewish Publication Society, 2019).

6 "No Religion is an Island," *Abraham Joshua Heschel: Essential Writings*, 116.

7 See "Carl Stern's Interview with Dr. Heschel," in *Moral Grandeur and Spiritual Audacity* (Farrar, Straus, and Giroux, 1997), 399. Heschel began thinking about issues of religion and justice much earlier in life, publishing poems on this theme as a teenager. In fact, his very first book was a bilingual collection of Yiddish poetry with an arresting title, *The Ineffable Name of God: Man*, trans. Morton M. Leifman (Continuum, 2007 [originally published in 1933]).

8 See, for example, the comments by Congressman John Lewis in Martin Doblmeier's 2021 documentary film, *Spiritual Audacity: The Abraham Joshua Heschel Story* (Journey Films).

9 "Religion and Race," *Abraham Joshua Heschel: Essential Writings*, 65.

10 This was an expression Dr. King used repeatedly. To learn more about the shared values and priorities of these modern prophetic figures, see Susannah Heschel, "Theological Affinities in the Writings of Abraham Joshua Heschel and Martin Luther King, Jr.," *Black Zion: African American Religious Encounters with Judaism*, ed. Yvonne Patricia Chireau and Nathaniel Deutsch (Oxford University Press, 2000), 168–186.

11 Abraham Joshua Heschel, *Man's Quest for God: Studies in Prayer and Symbolism* (Charles Scribner's Sons, 1954), 8.

12 See Heschel, *Man's Quest for God* and Abraham Joshua Heschel, *The Sabbath* (Farrar, Straus, and Giroux, 1951).

13 See "How John F. Kennedy Overcame Anti-Catholic Bias to Win the Presidency," *History*, https://www.history.com/news/jfk-catholic-president.

14 After further negotiation, the March on Washington did take place on August 28, 1963. This peaceful protest drew approximately 250,000 people and further galvanized the civil rights movement. In 1964, the Civil Rights Act was passed into law and in 1965 the Voting Rights

Act. See Lucy G. Barber, *Marching on Washington: The Forging of an American Political Tradition* (University of California Press, 2002).

15 Television commentator Melissa Harris-Perry quoted these words as part of an interview she conducted with Dr. Susannah Heschel and Rev. Jacqui Lewis in honor of the fiftieth anniversary of the Selma March: "John Lewis recounts memories of Bloody Sunday," *MSNBC*, March 8, 2015, https://www.msnbc.com/melissa-harris-perry/watch/john-lewis-recounts-memories-of-bloody-sunday-410061379607.

16 To learn about this concept, see Norman Lamm, "Worship Through Corporeality," *The Religious Thought of Hasidism* (Yeshiva University Press, 1999), 324–325. One striking image these mystical masters used was the need to seek out divine "sparks" throughout creation.

17 See Susannah Heschel's introduction to *Abraham Joshua Heschel: Essential Writings*, 35.

18 See Biale et al., *A New History of Hasidism*.

19 Edward Kaplan treats this subject extensively in *Spiritual Radical: Abraham Joshua Heschel in America* (Yale University Press, 2006), 235–276.

20 See note 5 and Alon Goshen Gottstein, "No Religion is an Island: Following the Trail Blazer," *Shofar* 26:1, 2007, 72–111.

21 See "Clergy and Laymen Concerned about Vietnam (CALCAV)," *The Martin Luther King, Jr. Research & Education Institute of Stanford University*, October 25, 1965, https://kinginstitute.stanford.edu/clergy-and-laymen-concerned-about-vietnam-calcav.

A Holy Exile

1 Robert Pear, "Falwell Denounces Tutu as a 'Phony,'" *New York Times*, August 21, 1985, https://www.nytimes.com/1985/08/21/world/falwell-denounces-tutu-as-a-phony.html.

2 Michael Battle, *Desmond Tutu: A Spiritual Biography of South Africa's Confessor* (Westminster John Knox, 2021).

Borders and Belonging: The Book of Ruth: A Story for Our Times

1 Padraig Ó Tuama and Glenn Jordan, *Borders and Belonging: The Book of Ruth: A Story for Our Times* (Canterbury Press, 2021), 4.

2 Ó Tuama and Jordan, *Borders and Belonging*, 8.

3 Ó Tuama and Jordan, *Borders and Belonging*, 9.

4 Ó Tuama and Jordan, *Borders and Belonging*, 9.

5 Ó Tuama and Jordan, *Borders and Belonging*, 22.
6 Ó Tuama and Jordan, *Borders and Belonging*, 45.

Oneing
An Alternative Orthodoxy

The biannual literary journal of the Center for Action and Contemplation.

> *The Perennial Tradition*, Vol. 1, No. 1, Spring 2013
>
> *Ripening*, Vol. 1, No. 2, Fall 2013
>
> *Transgression*, Vol. 2, No. 1, Spring 2014
>
> *Evidence*, Vol. 2, No. 2, Fall 2014
>
> *Emancipation*, Vol. 3, No. 1, Spring 2015
>
> *Innocence*, Vol. 3, No. 2, Fall 2015
>
> *Perfection*, Vol. 4, No. 1, Spring 2016
>
> *Evolutionary Thinking*, Vol. 4, No. 2, Fall 2016
>
> *Transformation*, Vol. 5, No. 1, Spring 2017
>
> *Politics and Religion*, Vol. 5, No. 2, Fall 2017
>
> *Anger*, Vol. 6, No. 1, Spring 2018
>
> *Unity and Diversity*, Vol. 6, No. 2, Fall 2018
>
> *The Universal Christ*, Vol. 7, No. 1, Spring 2019
>
> *The Future of Christianity*, Vol. 7, No. 2, Fall 2019
>
> *Liminal Space*, Vol. 8, No. 1, Spring 2020
>
> *Order, Disorder, Reorder*, Vol. 8, No. 2, Fall 2020
>
> *Trauma*, Vol. 9, No. 1, Spring 2021
>
> *The Cosmic Egg*, Vol. 9, No. 2, Fall 2021
>
> *Unveiled*, Vol. 10, No. 1, Spring 2022
>
> *Nonviolence*, Vol. 10, No. 2, Fall 2022
>
> *Transitions*, Vol. 11, No. 1, Spring 2023
>
> *Falling Upward*, Vol. 11, No. 2, Fall 2023
>
> *Art and Spirituality*, Vol. 12, No. 1, Spring 2024
>
> *The Path of the Prophet*, Vol. 12, No. 2, Fall 2024

Oneing is a limited-issue publication; therefore, some issues are no longer in print. To order available issues of *Oneing*, please visit https://store.cac.org/collections/oneing.

Center *for* Action *and* Contemplation